how to start a home-based

Online Retail Business

HOME-BASED BUSINESS SERIES

how to start a home-based

Online Retail Business second edition

Jeremy Shepherd
Revised and updated by Nicole L. Augenti, Esq.

Guilford, Connecticut

Copyright © 2007, 2012 Morris Book Publishing, LLC
Second Edition Printing 2012

Editorial Director: Cynthia Hughes Cullen
Editor: Katie Benoit
Project Editor: Tracee Williams
Text Design: Sheryl P. Kober
Layout: Justin Marciano

ISSN: 2162-0547
ISBN-13: 978-0-7627-6365-8

Printed in the United States of America
10 9 8 7 6 5 4 3 2 1

Contents

Acknowledgments

Author's

I would like to dedicate this book to my son, Jordan, who will someday take the reigns of the pearl empire.

I would like to thank Vivian for her endless support and patience while I completed this project and as I have grown with PearlParadise.com. Without her none of this would have been possible.

I would also like to thank Cori Amoroso for her months of tireless research and editing.

Revisor's

I would like to dedicate this book to my mom, Helen LoCascio, for believing in me—always.

I would like to thank James O. Gaston, Esq. for his endless support and for selflessly helping me run my law firm while I took the time to complete this book. I must thank the many online sellers (whom I also call friends) for helping to educate me on the world of e-commerce and for their support, energy, and enthusiasm for me to complete this book.

I would also like to thank my editors, Katie Benoit and Tracee Williams, contracts manager, Jessica Simons, and all the folks at GPP for their months of tireless research and editing and most importantly for their patience.

Introduction

In 2006 I was working full-time as a legal assistant as well as attending law school. One day, when I was supposed to be studying for exams, my mind wandered (as is typical for most people studying for anything) and I started thinking about selling on eBay. (After all, I had certainly made enough purchases from eBay sellers.) My original thought was that it would be a good idea to sell my textbooks when I was finished with them, but I have never been one to do anything small. Somehow, this seedling of an idea turned into an entire enterprise and within weeks I had purchased inventory and had a full-fledged eBay store up and running. It is no secret that law school is expensive and I realized having a second job to supplement my income—one that I could work from home, at any time of the day or night—would be a fantastic idea.

I have always been interested in fashion; in fact, buying $200 jeans from eBay sellers for $80 is how I became involved with eBay in the first place. If other people could sell designer apparel online, why couldn't I? Of course, I had to conduct diligent research to find inventory suppliers, but I firmly set my mind to it and I was successful.

The best part was that now I was getting my own clothes for less than wholesale prices—a double win! After about a year of selling only designer clothing and shoes, I decided to expand my new enterprise. I began to sell home decor items, with a particular emphasis on holiday items. I had two stores for a couple of years—one sold fashion apparel and the other, the home and holiday decor items. Not only was my online business helpful with paying the bills, but it was also much fun. It is a wonderful thing to have an income-producing business that feels more like a really fun hobby. I worked all the time (I still do) but the old adage is true: "If you love what you do, it isn't work."

If you decide to enter the world of online sales, it is vitally important that you remain constantly aware of market trends as well as the economic climate. I sold mostly expensive designer fashions from 2006 through 2009. In early 2009, as you will recall, the United States entered a rather catastrophic recession. I had the instant foresight to know that the high-end clothing that I was selling would no longer garner a profit. People were going to stop spending money, and if they were going to spend it, it was going to be far less often.

I decided right away to switch my inventory and entire focus of my business to the world of cosmetics. I knew that one thing that would deter online sales in a recession was high shipping prices. Cosmetics are very light and cost very little to ship, and I knew I was making the right decision. Once again, I had to find inventory suppliers and once again was successful. I changed the name of my business to "City Chic Style" and there it was, a booming wholesale cosmetics business virtually overnight. Your success will come from your own drive to be successful and from how much time and effort you are willing to put into your business.

One of the main reasons for the revision of this book is that it is crucial that you understand the role that social media plays if you want to have an online retail business in today's world. Something rather incredible happened while I already had my online sales business up and running and that was the explosion of social media—specifically sites like Facebook and Twitter—are essential tools that you need to utilize in order to maximize your success and exposure and ultimately carve out your own niche in the vast world that is the World Wide Web.

—Nicole L. Augenti, Esq. www.augentilaw.com

01 The ABCs of Starting an Online Business

When Jeremy Shepard first wrote this book, he implemented a lot of great information that he learned during his early days selling pearls online. A lot of that information is still very pertinent today. But as all things go, ever-changing modern technologies always affect the way we do business, and nothing has so impacted today's business like social media and the extensive growth of the Internet. When it came time for me to revise this book, I wanted to build upon the wonderful foundation that Jeremy built and add lessons I learned from my own experience. Look throughout for my "Expert Tip" sections. I presented my story in the introduction and now here is Jeremy's story.

Publisher's Note: Throughout the book you as the reader will benefit from both Nicole and Jeremy's expertise. Since the book was originally written by Jeremy Shepard and now revised by Nicole Augenti, there will be instances when each author is referring to his or her personal experience in the first person so please note the book is written with two distinct voices.

The Future of Online Retail

US e-commerce and online retail sales are projected to reach $197 billion in 2011, an increase of 12 percent over 2010.

—*Forecast of eCommerce Sales in 2011 and Beyond,*
www.fortune3.com/blog/2011/01/ecommerce-sales-2011/

How I Got Started

I was a flight attendant. I loved my job and it was fulfilling, to a point. See, I always felt as though I wanted more. Growing up, there were two "bugs" that were constant in my life—a love for travel and a strong entrepreneurial spirit. I started several small businesses as a child, most memorably a cookie business (I made and sold cookies), and a golf ball business (I dove for golf balls that golfers hit into the river and sold them back to the golfers). After attending high school in Japan for a few years, I moved back to Washington to live with my family, and the summer after I graduated from high school, I got a job working at a hotel. There I found a new way to fulfill my entrepreneurial ambitions. Amway had conventions in the city every summer, and the conventioneers always had problems with transportation from the hotel to the convention center. I often heard the conventioneers complaining about the price of cab fare. This gave me an idea. I started a shuttle service that transported the conventioneers from the hotel to the convention center and back. The shuttle service operated from 8:00 a.m. to 12:00 a.m. and I charged $5.00 per passenger. The conventioneers eagerly paid for the service because it was cheaper than taking a cab to the convention center. My new business was highly successful because there was a need for cheap transportation, and I filled that need. But after several years the travel bug started biting again, so I decided to take a job with Northwest Airlines. During a four-day layover in China in the winter of 1996, an opportunity presented itself. Shopping was a favorite pastime of most crew members, and the pearl market was a favorite shopping stop. I'd heard of the pearl market before, but I had no real desire to visit because my days were filled with trips to the Great Wall, Tiananmen Square, the Summer Palace, and other various stops suggested in my local guidebook.

During my last day in Beijing, I went to the pearl market with another group of flight attendants because I wanted to buy my girlfriend a strand of pearls. I selected a strand of what looked like nice pearls to me. Although I knew nothing about pearls at the time, I was still amazed at the low price—$25!

After giving the pearls to my girlfriend, she was curious about the US retail value of the pearls, so she took them to a local gemologist. Upon a detailed examination of the pearls, the gemologist produced a retail appraisal of the pearls with a valuation of $600. The pearls were worth thirty times what I had paid for them! This is when I knew that I had stumbled onto something. I didn't know how or where I was going to sell these pearls, but I cashed my paycheck from Northwest, took the next flight to China, and bought as much inventory as I could. You might say that I stuck my toe in the water and dove in headfirst. But one thing I've learned over the years is that successful entrepreneurs are those who have the ability to see an opportunity and the courage to act on the unknown. I wasn't sure where this was going to take me, but it was an opportunity I couldn't pass up.

Now that I had the product, where was I going to sell it? I took a chance on a very new retail space—the Internet.

The World Wide Web

The World Wide Web was still in its infancy in 1996, and e-commerce—transactions that take place electronically over the Internet—was just beginning to take off. The World Wide Web and e-commerce have undergone numerous changes since then. According to the Census Bureau of the Department of Commerce, in 2010 total US e-commerce sales reached $165.4 billion. There is no doubt that the popularity of online retail stores reflects consumer need for convenience and accessibility.

Facts

- The World Wide Web (WWW) was developed in 1989 by scientist Tim Berners-Lee of CERN (the European Organization for Nuclear Research), based in Switzerland.

- Berners-Lee, a graduate of Oxford University, got the idea for the WWW because he was frustrated that his telephone numbers, documents, and addresses were not easily accessible in one database.

- On April 30, 1993, the directors of CERN signed a document declaring the WWW free to everyone.

But back in 1996 I wasn't banking on the web taking off the way it eventually did. My decision was purely economical—I couldn't afford the rent of a retail store. Basically, selling on the web seemed cost-effective, and it didn't bind me to the rental lease of a brick-and-mortar retail space. Also, I thought it was cool to have a retail space that stayed in one place but availed itself to buyers around the world who wanted to see my product twenty-four hours a day, seven days a week. (Now, don't think that once you have established your website sales will immediately come your way. A website remains invisible until somebody knows it exists. Website visibility is something that I'll talk about in the upcoming chapters.) Since then, I've invested a tremendous amount of time nurturing my business. It was my special creation—from its conception to its birth. It has been everything to me, and now that my baby is approaching adolescence, many changes will occur as the market evolves and consumer needs change. But that's the great thing about being an online business owner: Nothing ever stays the same.

How to Explore Your Potential to Run a Home-Based Online Retail Business

If you've picked up this book, presumably you have already decided that you want to launch an online retail business. But do you really have what it takes to become an entrepreneur? This question isn't asked to burst your bubble. There is a philosophy that anything can be achieved with the right attitude—provided you are willing to do what is necessary to become successful. If you have the vision to do something great, you can learn and develop the knowledge and skills necessary to succeed in business. So before jumping in headfirst, let's make sure you've got a crystal clear image of where you are and where you want to go.

> "I highly recommend going to as many seller seminars as possible. Talking to other sellers while learning from the pros is the best way to stay motivated!"
> —*Michelle Gauvreau, Owner,* Ladystarres Treasure Cove,
> http://stores.shop.ebay.com/ladystarres-treasure-cove

First, it's important to assess your current situation. Like many people who start a home-based online retail business, you may be in one or more of the following situations:

- You are a stay-at-home parent.
- You have experienced a change in lifestyle requiring you to spend more time at home.
- You are in an unsatisfying work situation.
- You are worried about losing your job.
- You are looking to make a career change.
- You want to enhance your financial situation.
- You have discovered an innovative way to sell a product or service.
- You have created/designed a product you think will have market potential.
- You have discovered an excellent source from which to buy your product.
- You want to be your own boss.
- You want to be in control of your own time.
- You want to challenge yourself by seeking a new endeavor.
- You want greater control of your destiny.
- You want to make money doing something you love.

Next, ask yourself the following questions:

- How much time do I have to commit to this business?
- Do I have the financial resources to start an online business?
- How much knowledge do I have about the online business, marketing, sales, and Internet technology?
- How deep is my desire to take on such an endeavor?
- What obstacles do I have in my life that might prevent me from owning my own business?
- What is my passion?

Asking yourself the above questions will help you put things into perspective. It will also give you an understanding of what skills you need to cultivate.

This is a wonderful success story: "The inspiration for my natural and organic beauty line is my teenage daughter, Aubrey-Shea. She suffered from dry scalp, eczema, and acne outbreaks. I began researching natural alternatives to costly, chemical-laden medications and was not satisfied with anything I found. So, I decided to develop my own! Through countless hours of research and formulations, I developed this highly effective beauty line of products. I am happy to say that my daughter now has beautiful shiny hair, clear and balanced skin, and no more dry scalp. I offer hand-crafted all-natural and organic spa quality health and beauty products, such as hot and cold process artisan soaps, pure organic rose water, Dead Sea mud and salts, sugar scrubs, custom blended oils, anti-aging creams, and more. My favorite mediums to work with are the precious Moroccan Argan Oil and ancient secret of the Hawaiians Kukuinut Oil. I have been selling online since June 2009 and have learned a lot from a few great folks willing to share their expertise, including one of the authors of this book. Thanks Nicole!"

—*Patricia C. Cianflone, Owner/Formulator* of "THE Eco-Chic Boutique," http://theecochicboutique.etsy.com; http://theeco-chicboutique.com. Ms. Cianflone is also the author of a deliciously informative blog: http://theecochicboutique.wordpress.com.

The Elements of Success

Successful online entrepreneurs possess certain qualities that set them apart from others. Some might believe that having loads of money is the most important thing to starting a business. Not true. You can have an infinite amount of financing, but it's useless without the right attitude and perspective. Successful online entrepreneurs innately possess or have developed a series of characteristics that I call "Entrepreneurial Intelligence" (or "EI" for short). This allows them to be innovative thinkers and managers in today's technological climate. Perhaps you already possess these characteristics but just didn't know it. The key to success is in reflecting on your own values and attitudes so you can fairly assess where you stand in the Entrepreneurial Intelligence Quotient.

There are six elements to EI: Desire, Drive, Dedication, Awareness, Innovation, and Motivation. I have divided them into two sections. The first section is what I refer to as the **3-D** actions: **D**esire, **D**rive, and **D**edication:

Desire

When I went into the pearl business, it became my number-one priority, which meant that I wanted it more than anything else in the world. Setting up the business consumed my thoughts twenty-four hours a day. But I also knew that my desire had to graduate from mere thought to action—so I acted on it. I did the things necessary to set up my new business, and I transformed my dream into reality. Most people dream about what they want to do and never get around to doing it. The true test of desire is turning the idea into physical reality.

Drive

In the face of adversity, that driving force inside you will help you get through moments of uncertainty. Drive takes away ambiguity and replaces it with the energy to see things through. When I decided to buy pearls in China, I knew that I needed to learn everything there was to know about pearls, and I knew that I had to be able to communicate with the Chinese vendors. So I took a correspondence course through the Gemological Institute of America (GIA), and a Mandarin Chinese course through the Berlitz language school. Part of what drove me was the need to learn about my product and to develop the necessary communication skills.

Another key aspect of drive is patience. You need to understand that making a profit does not happen overnight. Most online entrepreneurs give up before they give their business a chance to see any profit. Successful entrepreneurs have enough drive to solve their problems instead of throwing in the towel.

"I have sold on eBay for several years but mostly just for pocket money. I worked for many years out of my home as an administrative assistant and employment recruiter. The business I worked for had to close and I was left at forty years old without a job. I have stayed at home working most of my life so I did not want to go back out into the 'working world.' I decided that I would sell on eBay and make it the source of my income. I sell vintage lingerie, men and women's vintage clothing, and accessories. I also carry designer clothing. I love the challenge of the hunt when it comes to finding great vintage items for resale."

—*Kathy Leonard,* eBay ID: kathy188, Store Name: Fancy Pantz Vintage, http://stores.ebay.com/fancy-pantz-vintage

Dedication

When you finally dedicate yourself to your dream, it will require your attention, time, and energy. Reflect on your past work ethic. How did you perform in your last job? Have you always had a good work ethic, or is this something that you need to develop? It is easy to be dedicated to something when things are going well, but true dedication is work ethic plus perseverance. Dedicating yourself to your business means that the leisurely activities you may have enjoyed in the past will take a backseat. Are you prepared for this? Is your family? It's important that those closest to you understand that from now on your online business will be your priority.

When I started PearlParadise.com I was already working full time, and building a company takes a great deal of time and energy. My decision to start the company meant I would forgo what little personal and leisure time I had left. It was only through sheer dedication that I built a successful online company.

The next three elements make up what I call the **A.I.M.** for success mentality: **A**wareness, **I**nnovation, and **M**otivation.

Awareness

Opportunity recognition is one of the most important aspects of becoming an entrepreneur. Once you determine that you are going to be an online entrepreneur, you must become a keen spectator of your surroundings. You never know when and where the next big idea will come. You might be offered an unbelievable deal or come across information about a great product source. Or sometimes opportunities come at you unexpectedly. In my case, I didn't realize the opportunity knocking at my door in that pearl market until I learned of the pearls' market value in the States. You can also create your own opportunity by being proactive. Knowing what's out there on the WWW is one way of being aware of your marketplace. Take a business class or a class that is related to your niche product. Read trade publications and journals in retail sales and about your product. Always be aware of future trends, and always be aware of your competition!

Innovation

Most entrepreneurs are always thinking of different ways to do things. Some online entrepreneurs are actually inventors who want to market and sell their own product. Some have found a product niche and have devised a savvy marketing strategy. Innovators are always looking for creative ways to solve problems in setting up and running an online business by thinking out of the box, by critically analyzing the problem in ways that have never been done before.

Reflect on your past experiences and assess how you might have come up with a creative way to solve a difficult problem. Being innovative is about seeing the possibilities that others don't see. You must be able to use innovative plans and solutions to make your business different from and better than the competition. So if you want to set yourself apart from the competition, study what they are doing right—then do it better.

> "Innovation is the specific tool of entrepreneurs, the means by which they exploit change as an opportunity for a different business or a different service. It is capable of being learned, capable of being practiced. Entrepreneurs need to search purposefully for the sources of innovation, the changes and their symptoms that indicate opportunities for successful innovation. And they need to know and to apply the principles of successful innovation."
>
> —Peter Drucker, *"The Father of Modern Management"*
> Source: Innovation and Entrepreneurship

Motivation

Motivation is that source of inspiration that will make you get up in the morning. On the days when I just wanted to stay in bed, it was motivation that forced me to haul my tired body back to the computer and telephone. Your dream to be successful and to make more money so that you and the people you care about can enjoy life to its fullest can be a source of motivation.

Okay, you're sure you've got what it takes. Are you sure online retailing is the way to go?

The Pros and Cons of an Online Retail Business

Yes, e-commerce is gaining popularity. People in remote areas can visit a site with just a click of the mouse. Online shopping is quick and convenient, and buyers can do it in the comfort of their home. This is why buyers and sellers are eager to get into the game of online retail. Amazon.com and eBay were the first to garner success in online retail, and individuals are quickly jumping on the bandwagon with their own websites. It is, however, important to delineate the pros and cons of starting an online business.

Pros

- Low start-up cost
- Ubiquitous web presence
- International access
- Business conducted 24/7
- Quick response to customers
- Low overhead = Lower product cost
- No more commuting

Cons

- No immediate visibility to your customers
- You can't see your customers
- Constant need to update website
- Late nights working from home
- Lack of inherent customer trust of a virtual entity
- Lack of health care benefits
- Disruption of business and family privacy

Some of the pros can make things complicated. For example, international access means that you have a potentially global customer base, but it also means that you need to be aware of the distinction between national and international shipping requirements. Some pros can also be cons, but knowing the difference between the online world and the brick-and-mortar world will help you maximize the benefits of owning an online retail store.

The Skills You Need

Most online entrepreneurs start out with a shoestring budget, so unless you just won the lottery or have some source of unlimited wealth, you should better be prepared to do as much as possible on your own. I'm not just talking about how to fix your own computer or how to design your own website, but other intrinsic skills, which may or may not come naturally to you. When I started my company I already had many business skills under my belt, but I lacked financial-planning skills. I succeeded because I recognized my weakness and took steps to learn more.

Nurturing Skills

You need to treat your online business as if it were your child. This attitude is one of the most important components needed to start and sustain a business. You need to love it, protect it, and help it evolve into a fully functioning entity. And you, the entrepreneur, will be the guiding force to that greatness. Starting your own online business

Expert Tip

Online selling does not have to be a full-time business. Some of you will want to sell part-time to supplement income, as a hobby, or for any other reason personal to you. I sold online while in law school and then while practicing as a lawyer while building my law firm. I was successful with it as a second job because I loved it and made sure to find the time to put in as much time as I needed to in order to sustain my business at the level I wanted it to be. I mastered the art of using Facebook and Twitter and other forms of social media as a result of having an online store. Social media skills are essential to most businesses or careers today. So even if you are just a part-time seller, if you dedicate yourself, you should always be learning something new that can help you in other areas of your life as well.

is like giving birth to a child and rearing it to realize its full potential. It will need your constant attention and protection as it starts out, your guidance when it starts to walk, and your wisdom to direct it to the right path. This is how I felt about Pearl Paradise.com. I had the same dreams and aspirations a father has for his child. I woke up early every morning to spend time with my company before leaving for work as a flight attendant, and I rushed home after work every day to immerse myself again.

Business Skills

Despite the fact that this new venture is your "baby," you must always be a rational and critical thinker when it comes to managing your business. You need to develop a working understanding of the daily aspects of running a business, such as follow-ups, budgeting, decision making, and shipping. The following is a list of skills you'll need in the daily aspects of running an online business:

- Basic accounting and bookkeeping
- Business communication (letters, memos, etc.)
- Negotiation
- Filing
- Multitasking
- Record keeping

Although you are following a dream, the nuts and bolts of business—which may not interest you that much—still need attention. I could have spent all of my time designing jewelry, bettering the website, and traveling the world in search of more pearls (the romantic part of my business), but without taking the time to keep records and financials, the company would have foundered.

Management Skills

How good are you at making decisions? Management is the ability to make reasonable decisions and to execute them in the most efficient way possible to achieve the maximum result. Although you might be a one-person team in the beginning, as your business grows you will begin to need help. Can you manage multiple personalities working for you? Can you objectively handle a delicate situation? Can you command the needed respect required to get people to follow you? Management skills are leadership skills. You need to exude the essence of credibility and dignity in managing not only your future employees, but also those you will be encountering in the course of your business. Good management is good leadership, and a good leader is a benevolent leader. Although you need to run a tight ship, employees who are happy with their boss are generally more productive and loyal.

When I hire a new employee I am not just looking for someone with the best credentials, I am looking for someone to be a part of the family. Every new member of the family is interviewed by the head of every department and by other key personnel. Although this is time-consuming, everyone plays an important role in the company. A good manager understands how certain personalities will mesh.

Organizational Skills

Once you start your business, you will become caught up in a whirlwind of events that will require your immediate attention. In other words, things can become a mess if you don't put them in the proper order. One way to organize is to understand the priorities of your daily events. You can organize them sequentially or according to importance. Develop a filing system that works for you and your business. If you have experience in an office environment, think about the filing system in that office. Was it efficient? Was it easy to follow? Can you adopt that system in your business? If you've never worked with or created a filing system before, you can simply make a list of all the different aspects of your business. Take this list and determine if any subcategories are necessary, and label a folder for each—a large folder for category topics, and small folders for subcategories. Depending on the number of files you amass, you may further break down the files by month.

Time planning is another important organization skill. You will need to schedule appointments, shipping deadlines, etc. Good organizational skills will help you keep everything in order and will prevent chaos. It may sound ridiculously low-tech, but I find that a to-do list is helpful because it serves as a reminder of the things I need to do on a particular day, and it feels great to cross out each item that I've completed. And since online retail can require a tremendous amount of shipping, being organized in that department by creating an efficient schedule will help you get your product out on time, which is crucial to maintaining good customer service.

Building your business will be very exciting, as it was for me, and you may have a to-do list a mile long with your dreams laid out in chronological order. Without good time management you will rapidly become overwhelmed. I have found it exceedingly useful to simply categorize tasks by priority, and to make sure each is fulfilled to satisfactory completion before starting another.

> "In my opinion there is nothing more important in your listings than good, clear photographs. There is a common saying out there among sellers that customers do not always read the descriptions—so arm yourself! Take pictures as if your buyer is not going to read your description because we all love to look at pictures and, after all, they speak a thousand words."
>
> —*Danni Ackerman, Owner,* Udderly Good Stuff, http://udderlygoodstuff.com, and on eBay: http://stores.ebay.com/udderly-good-stuff

Communication Skills

Just because you have an online business doesn't mean that you won't need to be an effective communicator. Remember that an online retail business is in many ways similar to the "brick-and-mortar" retail business. In the brick-and-mortar world, you show your customers the merchandise you want to sell. Effectively displaying your goods allows your potential buyers to see what you have to offer, and an attractive display makes your merchandise more appealing. Well, it is the same in the virtual world. Your website must effectively and beautifully communicate everything you have to offer. It must first appeal to your target market, and it must not intimidate people by overwhelming them with too much information.

Effective communication in the online world requires:

- Knowing your target audience
- Using words that your audience will understand ("keywords")
- Showcasing your product attractively
- Creating a reader-friendly website

Although these topics will be covered in upcoming chapters, I wanted to give you an overview of these elements, because part of your goal will be to convince the buyer that purchasing from your online retail store is the only way to go!

Communication has been a big part of my success. Developing a successful online company is always difficult, and in my case selling jewelry online without the benefit of the customer trying it on is challenging. But I did it. How did I do it? I was able to communicate directly to my customers through my website. In the beginning I conducted my own private market research using a personal focus group of family and friends. They gave me a good idea of what they would expect from me to entice them, or any customer, to purchase my product. For instance, I learned that detailed pictures, explicit product information, and strong guarantees helped garner customer interest and trust. My website is now focused on this core philosophy.

Expert Tip

The selection of a wrong or unrelated set of keywords will hamper the traffic flow through your website and will inversely affect the conversion rate of the site. It is also important to choose high demand keywords as your relevant keywords. High demand keywords on the search engines are those keywords that are most commonly searched by the surfers. Selecting less popular keywords again will not be effective in attracting influx to your website. For more on keywords see chapter 7.

Technical Skills

Most people are intimidated by this, but if you know how to use a computer—in other words, if you know how to point and click—then chances are you have some basic technical skills. Chapter 7 will discuss in detail the technical aspects of creating a website and the dynamics of e-commerce, but if you know the basics of Microsoft Word, Excel, etc., then all you need to do is build up your skills so that you can manipulate the various software you will need in your business. You can learn about the various software you will need by consulting with a web designer or doing some online research yourself. It will also help to learn the most commonly used Internet terms (see appendix C). You can build your technical skills in various ways:

- Obtain software manuals and do the practice exercises
- Play around with the programs in your computer
- Practice with the online and offline tutorials offered in most computer programs
- Take a class at a local community college or at an institution with a continuing education program

Don't ever be intimidated by technology; chances are you know more than you think. This may surprise you, but it is very likely that you have much better online technical skills than I did when I started PearlParadise.com. My computer skills were nearly limited to the on/off button of my computer. When I decided to build a website, I knew I had a lot to learn. I found an online tutorial, bought a couple of books, and went to work. I went from knowing absolutely nothing about computer programming to having a functional website in only seven days.

Are You Ready to Be an Online Entrepreneur?

Do You Have What It Takes?

- Desire
- Drive
- Dedication
- Awareness
- Innovation
- Motivation

Do You Have the Necessary Skills?

- Nurturing Skills
- Business Skills
- Management Skills
- Organizational Skills
- Communication Skills
- Technical Skills

What to Expect—What Not to Expect

Many online entrepreneurs get into the business because they believe that selling online is easier than having a conventional retail store. Online retailing has its advantages, but you shouldn't have unrealistic expectations about what you will be getting into. A big part of your success is in avoiding (when you can) the pitfalls of a new venture, but you can't do that if you're wearing rose-colored glasses. The most surprising thing I dealt with when I started selling pearls online was the scope of my customer base and the reach I would have. I had not anticipated receiving orders from every corner of the United States and from countries as far away as the Seychelles off the coast of East Africa. I had not expected the avalanche of 3:00 a.m. telephone calls, due to the time difference, from customers waiting for packages in Australia and from customers wanting to place orders from Germany. Remember, when you have an online business, the world is your customer base. An online business is a 24/7 business. This will never change.

Multitasking

Owning your own business requires that you wear many different hats—and sometimes it means wearing all the hats at the same time. As a new business owner, you'll often need to do everything yourself, and when things get busy, the constant bombardment of issues that need your immediate attention can be overwhelming. Multitasking is crucial to the successful online retailer. That's why it's so important that you get yourself organized and establish a working filing system—it will help you improve your aptitude for multitasking.

Most brick-and-mortar companies have several departments. Placing a telephone call to even a medium-sized company can often mean long waits and contact with four to five different departments before you find the department or people with whom you need to speak. When you begin your business you will be head of the sales department, shipping department, customer service department, and, of course, the complaints department. Managing all aspects of a business will require multitasking. When I was a flight attendant I managed shipping while at my home base, customer service and sales from my layover cities, and website design when most people were sleeping. I realized that every element was important and required direct concentration. You may not feel that multitasking is your strong point, but it is something that you will need to learn to develop because it is crucial, especially in the start of a business.

> "Multitasking can become much of a burden for many sellers. It's important that you utilize tools like a calendar or task manager or as simple as writing things down on paper or post-it notes to make sure you are not missing anything. It's better to do one thing really well than to do ten things only okay. Multitasking effectively is being able to dispense yourself in more than one direction with each project getting the same if not more of your effort as if you were only concentrating on one thing."
> —*Fredrick Nijm, CEO and Co-Founder* of Addoway.com, www.addoway.com

How Online Retailing Is Different from a Retail Store

If you already have a good understanding of retail sales, marketing, business, management, and customer service, then you're off to a great start (although you can start your online business without ever having worked a day behind a cash register). But online retail is still different from the brick-and-mortar store. Entrepreneurs who want to establish an online retail store should remember that how you showcase your product is not the only thing that differentiates you from brick-and-mortar retail. I'll talk about it in greater detail later, but below is a quick list.

- The *brick-and-mortar retail store* allows the customer to touch the merchandise.
- The *online retail store* must rely on pictures, graphics, and crafty product descriptions.
- Financial Planning: Brick-and-mortar stores require more capital due to rent or lease expenses.
- Location: The brick-and-mortar store is stationary, but an online store is ubiquitous. A brick-and-mortar is restricted by its geographical location in terms of customer traffic. However, local, national, and international customers can visit an online store.
- Communication: The brick-and-mortar store has the advantage of dealing with a potential customer on a face-to-face basis. Unfortunately, an online store communicates through text and graphics. This means that product pictures and product descriptions must accurately and efficiently communicate the merchandise to the buyer. The store must be able to answer all possible questions that a shopper might have about the merchandise by

presenting the item in such a way as to prevent any confusion about the product's size, price, and function.

- Technology: An online store relies on technology a great deal more than a brick-and-mortar store because the online retail environment changes according to the pace of technology, whereas brick-and-mortar stores have been around for hundreds of years.

Don't Count on Your Senses in the Virtual World

Shari Fitzpatrick of Shari's Berries (www.berries.com) is an online entrepreneur who has a successful online store that specializes in specialty desserts. Since the purchase of food items warrants that the buyer taste and smell the product, Shari Fitzpatrick has overcome the obstacle of the senses in the online retail world. According to Shari, the biggest difference between the online world and the brick-and-mortar world is customer service and labor cost. Online retail sites can stay competitive by offering great customer service, and they keep their costs down by saving on rent and labor. Her online store provides customers with great pictures of her products—so great that the mere look of it compels customers to buy. According to Shari, "the only thing offline has that online has not, is a great smell and a free sample of [her] products to encourage customers to buy."

Finding Your Niche

Perhaps the most challenging part of owning a business is deciding what kind of product or service to sell. One way to go about finding your niche is through a process of self-assessment. Ask yourself the following questions:

- What are my interests?
- What do I enjoy doing?
- What are my talents or skills?
- What sorts of products interest me?

After exploring the above, you will need to research the supply and demand of your product and create an innovative way of marketing it. One way to do this is by researching the competition. (I will talk about competition in chapter 12.)

Are You Ready to Become an Online Entrepreneur?

As I mentioned earlier, anyone can learn and develop the necessary skills to become an online entrepreneur. However, your biggest obstacle to success is fear and indecision.

Don't be afraid to take reasonable risks.

Don't fall prey to paralysis by analysis. Though a person can ruminate for years, the actual decision-making process takes just a split second. Rumination is good within reason, but don't psych yourself out of doing something great.

When I began my business I was excited by the possibility of the unknown. But I also loved the process of creating something tangible out of an idea that sprang from an unexpected opportunity. Reading this book will be your journey into the world of online retail, but I will also share with you my stories. I will share my successes and failures. I'm grateful for my successes, of course, but my mistakes are my most valued assets. They have taught me that success does not come without failure, and that failures are only detrimental if you don't learn from them. Most of all, being an entrepreneur is about surviving the ups and downs of running an online business, keeping the vision, and staying ahead of the competition. Business is a serious game, but it's a wonderful game and you can have a great time playing it so long as you have a passion for the game.

Advice for the Entrepreneur

10 Reasons Why Online Retail Entrepreneurs Make It Big	Top 10 Mistakes Online Entrepreneurs Make
1. Good product niche	1. Lack of product research
2. Good website design	2. Not finding a product niche
3. Excellent customer service	3. Lack of familiarity with online retail
4. Good market research	4. Poor website design
5. Competitive prices	5. Lack of financial planning
6. Innovative marketing	6. Poor customer service
7. Established word-of-mouth buzz	7. Ignorance of online legal issues
8. Good product sourcing	8. Lack of competitive edge
9. Good business and financial planning	9. Lack of commitment
10. They never lose their entrepreneurial spirit	10. Lack of passion

02 | The Home Office

An important step in launching your home-based retail business on the web is to make sure that you have a functioning work environment. After completing your self-assessment, it's important to conduct a thorough assessment of your living space. Many Internet moguls such as Bill Gates and Michael Dell started their business in their dormitory rooms. Start-up businesses can consult with www.sba.gov or a service like www.networksolutions.com for advice. Small businesses often begin with limited budgets and limited space, but these limits are temporary, and creating a functioning working space is essential. Your home, no matter how small, can be transformed into an efficient home office.

Carving Out Your Space

There are benefits to having your business at home. Living where you work is cost-efficient and convenient. You don't have to fight traffic because you don't have to worry about being late, and there's no dress code—you can have casual Friday every day. The most beneficial aspect of a home office is that you don't have to pay rental fees. So take a moment to assess your home environment and see its possibilities. If you live in a small space, check the nooks and crannies and you just might see a space for a file cabinet or a small desk. If you want to work out of your room, imagine how you can organize it to separate your personal items from your office supplies. Working out of your garage means that you can have some privacy and ample space for inventory. Sometimes a particular portion of your home environment will do double duty. Your kitchen can be your office during the day and a place to serve meals at night. It's incredible how many uses a kitchen table can have, from doing paperwork to shipping merchandise.

Developing a new attitude about your home surroundings will help you transform your domestic space into a professional environment that can become the breeding ground of your success. You should be motivated enough to want to organize your space, because pleasant working surroundings help you maintain a positive and productive attitude. The excitement about actually having an office space within your home should be enough for you to come up with innovative ways to transform your home.

All it takes is a little imagination and organization. A good way to start is by asking yourself the following questions about your home. Is it a small space, or do you have the option of converting a room, basement, or garage into a work space? Can you efficiently use walls to save floor space with wall units? Think of the nature of your business. How much inventory space will you need? If you have children or live with others, is there a quiet spot where you can work undisturbed? These questions will help you understand your current living situation, and they will help you with the modifications you will need to make to create a comfortable, functional, and efficient home office.

Freedom to Set Your Own Hours

Ryan Totka is a founding partner of TornadoPromotions.com, an online marketing and search engine optimization website that blends Totka's love of sports and his knowledge of e-commerce. Totka started his career as an entrepreneur when he launched CollegeInvestors.com when he was still a college student. He launched CollegeInvestors.com during the stock market boom. It was a website that educated college students on the fundamentals of stocks and investing. When the stock market ceased to be a profitable endeavor, Totka took the knowledge he gained from CollegeInvestors.com to TornadoPromotions.com and various successful e-commerce sites. Totka started his business as a home-based business. Totka loved the flexible hours of working at home. He also admits that having his business at home during those years meant long hours because "you live in your office," which means that working hours are as flexible as your sleeping schedule will allow. According to Totka, having an office means limited work hours (usually 9:00 to 5:00), but working from home means that one can work until 4:00 a.m.

Here are a few tips that should help you when scoping out your work space:

- Choose an area of the house that is quiet.
- Make sure that you have a convenient access to plugs and outlets.
- Consider any unused spaces such as garage, attic, or basement.

Expert Tip

I started my own online business at my desk in the corner of my bedroom (while my cat looked on intently from the foot of the bed). However, at the time, I was living in a one-bedroom apartment and since my inventory of choice was apparel, I quickly realized I needed more storage space (as visitors to my apartment were not very comfortable sitting on boxes). I moved to a two-bedroom apartment shortly after starting my business so that I would have a special room to exclusively store my inventory (eBay sellers refer to this special room as "the eBay room").

Setting Up Your Home Office

Transforming Your Old Space

How do you turn your old space into a new and exciting working environment? The first thing you will need to do is organize, so throw away or store away any unnecessary items or objects that you haven't used or haven't needed in the last few years. My rule is that if I haven't used it in two years, it goes in the trash or is donated to a local charity. If you already have a desk make sure you organize it by separating your "work papers" from everything else. If you don't have a desk, modular desks are economical. Simply buy a tabletop and place it above two small filing cabinets. Wall units are also very useful in small spaces. Using different color file folders for household business and your online business is one way to prevent mix-ups, especially when you might have to store business and personal information in the same cabinet.

My Humble Beginnings

When I started my online company, my dining room became my office. My computer was set on a small table, and all I needed was enough space for the computer, a printer, and a credit card machine. (In 1996 online orders were usually processed through a credit card machine. Today, most orders are processed online.) Because my product was small—pearls—I didn't need a lot of space for storage, either. I kept my inventory in a duffel bag inside my closet.

But as your business grows, your office must accommodate the increasing inventory and storage space you will need. In the beginning, I used little pouches for my pearls. Now that the business has grown, I use actual jewelry boxes, which means that I eventually had to accommodate my existing space to store the boxes.

Furthermore, I didn't even install an extra telephone line because I used my cell phone for all my business transactions; this way I could leave town—I was still a flight attendant—and still receive orders from customers, and they were always able to reach me. I took their payments over the phone, and I would process the credit card transaction when I got home. Credit card payments are processed automatically now, but back then you had to do it yourself. As you can see, I wore many hats when I first got started.

Expert Tip

If your intention is to be a casual seller or to exclusively conduct your business on a shared venue site, such as eBay, Amazon, Etsy, or Addoway, don't be scared off by some of the large (costly) items you read about in this chapter as you will not need a credit card machine, fax machine, or copy machine if you do not own your own website.

Economize

Deciding that you want to start your own business doesn't mean you have to spend a lot of money. The key is to get the most out of what you have. You will be surprised how much money you can save by being a smart shopper. Try to buy items on sale when shopping for office supplies. Seek out vendors that give discounts. And only buy the bare necessities, such as paper, printer ink, envelopes, paper clips, stapler, staples, etc. Sometimes buying in bulk is more economical in the long run, but that also depends on the nature of your business. If you're going to be doing lots of shipping, you'll need to buy the proper envelopes or boxes to ship your product, and it is more economical to seek out vendors that give discounts on items that you will be constantly using.

Equipment and Supplies

I started my home business with a computer, a printer, and a credit card machine. But as the business grew, I realized that I needed to invest in office equipment such as a copy machine and a fax machine. Though I was frustrated by my shoestring budget, it also allowed me to be resourceful. For example, because I lived in a small space at the time, I turned my kitchen into a work space. My kitchen table became my desk for processing orders, paying bills, and shipping my merchandise. I utilized every available space I had as storage for my inventory, packaging supplies, and office equipment. My limited budget meant that to save money I had to buy in bulk, and I stored boxes in closets and under the bed. Big boxes that couldn't be put away became work spaces by doubling as extra tables. In other words, I had a cramped but efficient working environment.

You might need additional equipment if you plan to make the product yourself. For example, if you're selling custom-made apparel, you might need to purchase a sewing machine. The garage is a good place to store heavy equipment, and it can also make a good office space.

Business Essentials

- Printer

- Digital camera

- Appropriate software products (QuickBooks, Word, Excel, etc.)

- Invoices (if you are selling on a shared-venue site such as eBay or Amazon or using PayPal or Google checkout to complete transactions, invoices are provided by those sites)

- Business cards and/or postcards, which include your site and associated pages, which are then included in your packages to customers

- Shipping and packaging supplies

- Facebook fan page

- Twitter page

- Other social media sites of choice

The advantage of using a cell phone in a home-based business is that it allowed me to do business in and out of the house. I was able to go out of town and still be accessible to customers or vendors. I could place phone orders to vendors and process customer orders when I was away from home. When I was a flight attendant, I took and processed orders in between flights.

Must Haves

Just because you work out of your home doesn't mean that you won't need to make certain necessary purchases. You'll definitely need a computer. If your computer belongs in the Smithsonian, you might want to think about buying a new one that will be able to accommodate DSL or cable Internet connection. Think about the

---

Must Haves Worksheet

In the space below make a list of the items that you must have, and then give them an approximate price. This should help you determine a preliminary budget.

_____	$_____
_____	$_____
_____	$_____
_____	$_____
_____	$_____
_____	$_____
_____	$_____
_____	$_____
_____	$_____
_____	$_____
_____	$_____
Total	$_____

product you want to sell, and determine your necessary expenses from that standpoint. It is a good idea to make a list of supplies you'll need. A list of "Must Haves" and "Can Do Withouts" can help you in making certain decisions about how you should budget. Below is a template of a "Must Have" list. Fill it out to determine the approximate amount of your initial expenditures.

Be realistic when making your list. Remember that a color copy machine is not really a necessary expenditure so long as there are places that can make the copies for you. Be cheap, but also be aware that there are just some things that you can't skimp on.

Tax Breaks

Having a home-based online business can offer you some tax breaks. If your office space is exclusively used for business on a full-time basis, then you are entitled to a tax break. You can obtain tax form 8829 to claim the deduction. To determine the amount of deduction, calculate your home or apartment's total square footage, then figure out the square footage of your office space. You can deduct the proportion of your office space from your mortgage principal or rent. For example, if your living space is 2,000 square feet and you use 250 square feet of that space for business, then the amount of rent or mortgage you pay for that particular office space is tax deductible. For added measure, take a picture of your home as a form of backup documentation in the event of an audit.

Formula for Computing Tax Write-Off for Office Space

Space = 2,000 square feet

Office Space = 500 square feet (¼ of total space)

Rent/Mortgage = $1,000

Amount of Deduction = $250

Rent/Mortgage ÷ Space = $ per square foot

$ per square foot x Office Space = Amount of Deduction

Insurance

It might also be a good idea to obtain insurance. If you're a homeowner, an endorsement from your homeowner's insurance policy can be obtained for equipment and/or liability, and the premium difference is fairly affordable. Insurance makes good business sense in the event of an accident, fire, or even if your computer breaks down. Check your policy to see if it offers a combined homeowner's and business policy program.

Other Expenses

Contact your local phone company for special home-business rates available to you. Remember that frugality can get you further than extravagance, and being "tight" is the name of the game for many start-up businesses.

Practical Tips

- Always be organized.
- Don't invest in unnecessary equipment or luxury office items.
- Stay within your budget.
- Try to find a functional place in your home where you can work undisturbed.
- Set up a simple yet efficient shipping system.
- Separate home-related business from your online business.
- Set up a work station that is convenient and manageable for you.
- Check for discounts that you may qualify for in your home office.

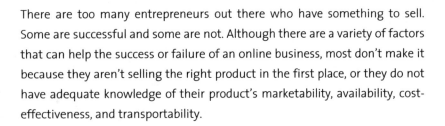

03 Finding Your Niche

There are too many entrepreneurs out there who have something to sell. Some are successful and some are not. Although there are a variety of factors that can help the success or failure of an online business, most don't make it because they aren't selling the right product in the first place, or they do not have adequate knowledge of their product's marketability, availability, cost-effectiveness, and transportability.

Marketability: Can you market your product online?
Availability: Can you find a good source for your product?
Cost-Effectiveness: Can you sell the product and make a reasonable profit?
Transportability: Can you ship your product easily?

I mentioned earlier that many online entrepreneurs get started through a hobby. Perhaps you've been interested in origami for years and you decide to start an online business selling origami supplies. Or maybe you're a car aficionado and you think that selling rare car parts online might be lucrative. Or maybe you've been working for a paper manufacturer or supplier for years and you know the ins and outs of the paper supply business, so you decide to start a business. The advantage of being a hobbyist and an experienced individual in a certain field is "knowledge." Having prior knowledge or experience about the product is important because it is better to sell what you know.

Then again, you might be like me—I discovered my product by sheer accident. I didn't know that a trip to a pearl market in Beijing would change the way I see and think about pearls. When I found out that buying pearls in China and selling them in the United States constituted a 50–100 percent markup, I knew that I had to go into business and that I had found a niche by selling my pearls online.

Discovering the Right Product to Sell

It is important that you start small when determining your product niche. I started by selling freshwater pearls because they were the least expensive type of pearls. They are the most common type of pearl, and they are available in a variety of colors and sizes. Finding your product niche begins with determining if the product is a good fit for you. In my case I never thought about, nor did I have an initial interest in pearls, until I realized how much money I could make by selling them. But since then, I have developed an avid appetite to know as much as I can about pearls. I have become a pearl expert because the more I learned about pearls, the more I wanted to know. Although pearls were not my original passion, it turns out that online pearl selling was a good fit for me because of two passions I already did have: foreign languages and travel. Being a pearl seller meant traveling to China, Hong Kong, French Polynesia, Australia, Indonesia, and Japan. I also needed to communicate with my vendors, and while I already spoke fluent Japanese, I studied Mandarin so I could communicate with the pearl farmers directly. My love for travel and my interest in language helped me fit into the role of being a pearl buyer and seller. The product has to fit you, but you also have to fit the product.

So, in determining you product niche, think about the following questions:

- Do you have any special interests or hobbies?
- How much knowledge do you have about your special interests or hobbies?
- Are you the type of person who is willing to do the research needed to adequately educate yourself about your prospective product?
- If you are currently working for a company, is there anything about your job that might give you some insight on what kind of product to sell?
- Do you have special knowledge about acquiring a particular product that might help you stay competitive in the online market?
- What is the life span of the product you have in mind?
- Is the product seasonal or will it sell all year long?

- Who do you think would buy your product?
- What is the market saturation of this product?
- How would you be able to market your product differently from your competitors?
- Do you have genuine interest in the product?
- Do you have a passion for the product?

Online retailers usually find success in selling products that are not too burdensome to ship, such as CDs, DVDs, clothing, shoes, accessories, jewelry, computer accessories, and novelty items. Avoid a product that has a high cost-to-shipping ratio. Although there is a market for televisions and exercise equipment, shipping such heavy-weight products is burdensome. Nevertheless, it is up to you to work out the kinks in whatever product you want to sell. One option is to drop ship the merchandise to avoid the hassle of packaging it yourself and warehousing costly inventory. Drop shipping occurs when a retailer receives an order for merchandise; the retailer then directs the order to the wholesaler who ships the goods directly to the buyer. The problem with drop shipping is that many other retailers are probably going through the same wholesaler, so establishing a product niche is difficult using this method.

"I sell dollhouse miniatures, artisan made dollhouse minis, and other collectibles. I have always loved miniatures ever since I was a child. I was fascinated by the books *Thumbelina, The Indian in the Cupboard,* and *The Borrowers.* I also loved stories about fairies, wee folk, and little people, such as *Rip Van Winkle.* I have a very creative and artistic bent and so I can make almost anything. I have been crafting dollhouse miniatures since I was only seven or eight years old. I particularly like to work with natural materials such as plants, wood, herbs, and moss—these items create incredibly detailed houseplants! We miniaturists have a saying: 'Is there anything in life that does not exist in miniature?'"

—*Roxanne Mitchell, Owner,* Heirloom Productions, Inc.
on Bonanza.com, www.bonanza.com/roxannmi

Learning about the Product

Although I didn't know anything about pearls, I knew that I had to learn about them if I wanted to convey credibility, not only to my customers, but to suppliers as well. Now I am a true pearl expert. One of the advantages of knowing about your product is that you decrease the risk of vendors and suppliers cheating you over product quality and price. And when I am on a buying trip to Asia, I know how to distinguish the quality of pearls because I've done my research. Moreover, you should be an expert on the product you are selling because that is one way you can keep your competitive edge. I'm continually reading books about pearls, and I'm constantly trying to find new information about the pearl market. Almost every product has its own variety of publications and trade journals available online and offline. Trade journals can be very valuable to you when it comes to product information. You can acquire empirical experience with your product or you can go to school. Universities and colleges can be expensive. You may apply for a student loan, but if you can't qualify for a loan, a community college is a good, affordable alternative. Or you can research on your own. It really doesn't matter how you acquire your knowledge, so long as you learn and your source of information is credible.

Expert Tip

I found the Internet to be my best friend for conducting market research. When I switched from selling apparel to selling cosmetics, it was still important to stay on top of the trends. For example, if white eyeliner was the current hot item then I made sure to have white eyeliner in stock and also made sure to sell it at appropriate market prices. Never forget: Along with researching the products themselves, it is equally important to research pricing.

Correspondence Courses

I am a big fan of correspondence courses because, in my opinion, they are really geared for busy individuals who want to learn at their own pace. Conventional schooling can be slow-paced and the student has to go by the instructor's lesson plans. Moreover, people with full-time jobs often find it hard to take night classes after a full day of work.

> "I run the local eBay/eCommerce Sellers Group in West Hartford, Connecticut. I have been an avid seller (and buyer) on eBay since 2001. I thoroughly enjoy making extra money and finding that 'wow' factor to sell. Talking to other sellers motivates me to stay in the game and I've learned so much. My learning prompted me to start my local group and we are growing by leaps and bounds. My motto for the group: Become educated about online selling."
> —*Michelle Gauvreau, Founder,* CT eBay and eCommerce Sellers Group, www.meetup.com/ct-ebay-and-ecommerce-sellers-group/

Correspondence courses are available everywhere and they allow you to study on your own time instead of on somebody else's schedule. Many entrepreneurs are educated through empirical experience, and the beauty of a correspondence course is its flexibility in allowing you to pick and choose courses that are applicable to your situation. The best kind of learning is when you can readily apply your knowledge to your immediate situation.

> "Working from home, it's easy to isolate yourself and not feel a part of something bigger. Make time to get involved in local meet-up groups and attend the larger conventions and functions where you can connect with people you have met online!"
> —*Danni Ackerman, Owner,* Udderly Good Stuff, www.udderlygoodstuff.com, and also can be found on eBay at: http://stores.ebay.com/udderly-good-stuff

There are also many local chapters that have been started by online sellers for the sole purpose of bringing online sellers together to share and learn from each other's experiences. If you are part of a shared venue site, ask on the message boards to see if any groups or "meet-ups" have been formed in your area.

Education

Many entrepreneurs believe education is not restricted to the classroom. Empirical experience is priceless, and there's nothing wrong with getting paid as you learn. Shari Fitzpatrick, founder of Shari's Berries (Berries.com), belongs to that school of thinking where knowledge through experience is the best kind of education one can receive. As a regular guest speaker at Sacramento State University's Entrepreneur Business Class, she always gets a big laugh from the students when she mentions that she hasn't taken a business class. Remember that being an entrepreneur is about being a leader, and sometimes leadership is learned on your own time and on your own terms. As for me, I do believe in education, but it is education through the various facets of life's experiences that will ultimately be the touchstone of your knowledge. Gut instinct has really been my greatest asset, and no one can teach you that.

Determining Product Demand and Availability

Know the demand for your product and the available sources for it. In other words, who is your target customer, and how can you acquire the product you want to sell? If you've invented a great product that you want to sell online, you will need to know how you can acquire the goods or parts that you will need to make your product. If you've decided that you want to sell books or DVDs, where can you get the best possible price to compete with other online sellers selling the same thing? The first way to do this is to check out who is interested in the product. You can tap into a specialized section such as rare or out-of-print books, for instance. If you sell something that very few people are selling, you limit your competition despite the small market of the product. Find out the target demographic of your product. This will also help you in designing your website because you can create a website that will "speak" to your target audience.

Second, research the suppliers of the product and find out to whom they are selling. Each major city will have various districts. For example, Los Angeles has the toy district and a garment district within blocks of each other. There, retailers can purchase directly from the distributors or possibly a manufacturer of toys and/or garments. But what you want to do is find out who the distributors are buying from so that you can talk straight to the source. You might not be able to purchase the product at the price you want, but you will establish a relationship with these vendors, and that is a start to developing your own leads and relationships with vendors.

How I Researched My Product

When I got into the pearl industry, I researched numerous jewelry stores to see the type of pearls they sold, the design of the jewelry, and their prices. I also talked to various jewelers about customer demand. In the beginning, I found out that there were just too many jewelry stores selling pearls, and the capital needed to open a jewelry store was too costly.

Then a friend introduced me to a couple of auction sites— Amazon.com and eBay.com. After researching the sites, I found out that there was little to no competition in those markets for selling pearls. So, with neither a digital camera nor the skills to scan a photograph, I listed my pearls (without a picture) for auction. I was pretty thorough in my description, and I listed the appraised market price for the pearls, which was $600, and my sale price for the pearls, which was $80. I listed them as a Dutch auction (multiple-item auction) for twenty sets. I received numerous bids the first day. That's how I knew that there was a market for my pearls.

The Lesson Learned:

I realized that market research is important. Although there seemed to be no place for my pearls in an oversaturated brick-and-mortar pearl market, there was plenty of room for them in the online world. Online retail has evolved since I started my business over ten years ago, but it is still a fairly young market, and there are many opportunities to be had. While online retail is no longer a novel idea, social media is still very young, and the combination of the two when used correctly is what makes this a particularly exciting time to venture into the world of online sales.

Sourcing Your Product

Sourcing your product is the process of finding a supplier that you can buy merchandise from at the most competitive prices. Regardless of what you are selling, you will either need to buy supplies for the manufacturing of your product, or you will need to buy the actual product itself from the manufacturer. Good sourcing is finding quality product at the price that you can afford. You can source domestically or overseas. Domestic sourcing is convenient and easy. You don't have to deal with language barriers or overseas shipping, and if you're a good negotiator, you can easily establish a relationship with a vendor. It is easy to get to know a vendor who is a mere car ride away. The only problem with domestic sourcing is the price. Most domestic vendors probably buy overseas, so you're not always getting the best deal. However, there are many products out there that are still manufactured in the United States and perhaps even in your local area.

On the other hand, the big advantage of overseas sourcing is the price. Things made in India and China are always cheaper when compared to things made in the United States. China and Hong Kong are meccas of manufacturing, and prices are phenomenally low. They host some of the largest trade shows in the world where factories from all over mainland China get together to show their wares or show what types of products they can produce. These are not small events, and I would liken visiting a large trade show in China or Hong Kong to walking through the Louvre in Paris—you can walk for days and still not see everything. Thousands of factory representatives in these trade shows man small booths with a myriad of products. Many of these products are already being imported here in the West, but many are not! It is up to you to have a keen eye in seeing the potential of a product when visiting these trade shows. Keep in mind that these overseas trade shows are very similar to the trade shows in the United States, except the prices in overseas trade shows will usually be lower.

Expert Tip

You must be extremely diligent when choosing your sources, whether they are located inside or outside of the United States. It is particularly important that if you choose to sell items that are heavily counterfeited, such as designer apparel or DVDs, that you know your product well, so that you can be certain you are not purchasing fakes or knock-offs for resale. Unfortunately, it is all too easy to locate a "really great deal" on inventory you want, but the old adage is true: "If it looks too good to be true, it probably is." This is why it is important to buy only a small "test" sample of items that are known to be heavily counterfeited, so that you can make sure the items you have purchased for resale are authentic. It should come as no secret that selling counterfeit items is illegal and claiming you were unaware that it was fake is no defense.

Because trade shows usually run for about a week, you will have time to do some research. Spend one or two days just browsing. Look for products that catch your eye, or if you already have a product in mind, look for vendors who are selling your product of interest. Then put together a possible list of vendors with their product list, minimum order quantities, and lead times (time for order placement to fulfillment), along with the "listed" price of the goods they're selling. Remember that these listed prices are not etched in stone—there is always room for negotiation. Once you've established your list, do some online research and check out who's selling similar items and how much they're selling for. I also suggest researching eBay for the same product to see how much it's selling for there. After doing this, place the products in order of preference. Which products would seem more appealing and appear to have the best chance of online success? Good products to sell online are products that do not require high shipping costs (high value-to-weight ratio), so large products like exercise equipment would probably not be that appealing, unless you can give the customer a really reduced price on the item. Once you've established the product, then you can go back to the trade show and start talking to the vendors. Some vendors will allow you to place sample orders of their products, which means that you can order below their minimum quantity. You can do this with various vendors and then test your product by selling it on eBay. eBay is a great testing ground, but be aware of their various fees. It can be a good place to start, but you may not want to stay there. The good thing about this site is that you have an immediate venue to test market your product.

Changing Suppliers

Changing suppliers can be a difficult task, especially if you've grown accustomed to your current supplier. Starting a new business relationship is difficult, but it is sometimes necessary and beneficial. As your business grows and as new competition inhabits your market, you will eventually have to change suppliers if your old one can no longer meet your demand for products. As I mentioned before, my first source for buying pearls was the Beijing pearl market. Even though there were hundreds of pearl traders there, I concentrated on finding one honest trader. I actually found one that I was comfortable with and we began negotiations. I bought from this merchant for almost two years because my gut instinct told me that he was reliable and he was someone I could do business with. It's rather difficult to delineate how you can find a supplier that you feel comfortable with. Most of this process will probably delve into your gut feeling about the supplier and the situation. You might also want to ask yourself how you feel about the supplier's personality and initial character. If you feel uncomfortable about doing business with a particular supplier, then do not do business with that supplier. Remember to trust your instinct about people, because you really will not have the opportunity to get to know the supplier personally, so the only gauge you have is your initial reaction to the person. When you're at the threshold of doing business with somebody, you should involve yourself with people whom you "feel" you can trust. For example, if your instincts tell you that you don't want to do business with a particular supplier, it would behoove you to pay attention to your hunches. Chances are that you are sensing a negative energy about that person. You might be able to prove your instincts, but I fully believe that first impressions are important; they are a sign you might encounter future problems with that vendor, or that your personalities might conflict. Indeed, business is business, but you should give your business to a company/individual that you feel comfortable with.

Nevertheless, once you find a good supplier and you begin to buy from that supplier regularly, there will eventually come a time when you see the need to find a new supplier. When this happened to me, I noticed that there was an influx of websites selling pearls in the United States. Most of my competitors sourced from the same place I bought my merchandise—the Beijing pearl market. I wanted to set myself apart from my competition, so I needed to find better sources for higher-quality pearls.

I had done some research on pearl farming and pearl factory locations, and I knew in which parts of China the freshwater and Akoya pearls—much higher-quality pearls than could be found in Beijing—were farmed and processed. They were usually in the remote areas (the provinces and the countryside), and the pearl factory managers rarely spoke English. I didn't speak Chinese at the time, so this is when I decided to enroll in the Berlitz language school. I took a three-month intensive language-training program. Throughout those three months I was focused on being able to communicate with the pearl factories in China so that I could stay in control of the negotiations rather than having to rely on a translator. I knew that this was one way to secure my product niche in the pearl industry. Getting higher-quality pearls for less directly from the source was my goal because none of my competitors actually bought directly from the source.

Choosing the Right Product for You

Choose a product that is affordable and accessible to you. Just remember that you must also be able to create a market demand and a niche for your product. It is also enough that your extensive knowledge of a product gives you an edge whereby you think you can compete with the market demand.

Eliminating the Middleman

After completing the Berlitz course, I continued researching the pearl farms in China. What I learned is that the farmers didn't typically sell directly to people like me—they sold to factories. These factories would then process the pearls and sell them to traders. These traders would take the pearls to places like the Beijing pearl market and sell them to the merchants that sold them again to people like me. Going directly to the pearl factories and being able to communicate with them in their native language meant that I could cut my cost and secure higher-quality pearls. Another important discovery I made was that some of the pearl farmers owned factories themselves, thus cutting out the middleman (the factories), which meant that their prices were much more competitive than the traditional factories that had to go to the pearl farmers themselves. I learned a very important lesson about cutting out the middleman—the cheapest way to buy your product is directly from the source.

My trip to the pearl farms was intimidating at first. I had to travel to the remotest part of South China, catch a rickety boat from Hainan, and figure out my way to one of the many "pearling" cities along the coast. My conversational and technical Chinese was, by then, good enough to communicate with the pearl farmers. I spent two weeks visiting the various factories there. Now I was not only able to select the absolute highest-quality pearls produced (in the Beijing pearl market there were times when I had no choice but to simply settle for what was currently available), but I was paying much less than I had previously paid for inferior pearls.

The Pros and Cons of Eliminating the Middleman

Pros

- Cutting your costs
- Paying less for more
- Extra revenue to invest in other aspects of your business
- Improved product quality

Cons

- Building a relationship with a new but unknown supplier
- Traveling to unknown territory

Negotiation

Negotiation is a key element in any business. Whether it is with suppliers, customers, or employees, a successful business will depend on your negotiation skills. When negotiating with suppliers, it is always in your best interest to be in a position where they need to sell more than you need to buy. Unfortunately, this is not always the case, but it's important not to show your eagerness. If you walk into a room showing too much interest in the merchandise, the supplier will demand a higher price. This doesn't mean that you should sneer or insult the product with the pretense of disinterest. It would not behoove you to offend a supplier, nor would it be good business form—always be polite. The important thing is to keep your cool.

A general approach I used to take with new suppliers was to never accept a price higher than only 30 percent of their initial asking price. This worked well for some time, but as I became better known in the Chinese pearl industry, they knew what I was willing to pay, and negotiation became just a formality. You should have a general idea of the wholesale price of the product, and in negotiating, never pay more than you can afford.

Negotiation is an important part of any business transaction, especially if you are dealing with a new supplier. I've already mentioned that it is best not to appear too eager to buy. But the most valuable device in negotiation is the true walk-away. If a supplier's prices are too unreasonable, there is nothing you can do but walk away. Sometimes, however, you are put in a situation where the supplier has the upper hand. Perhaps this particular supplier carries good-quality merchandise and there's no good substitute. In some cases, suppliers like to drag customers by the tail. They prolong the negotiations, hoping that the customer will relent to their prices. So the customer will pay the supplier's demands because sources for merchandise may be limited or the quality of the supplier's product is too top notch to pass up. This can put the retailer in a precarious situation. Although you might walk out of the deal with a "fair" price, you have the gut feeling that you should have been able to get better prices for the merchandise. So, you deal with this supplier for months, even years, because you are somehow trapped into the situation. You could look for another vendor, but you don't really want to—you just want lower prices from this particular vendor. What can you do?

Walking away from a negotiation might not pay off immediately, but it will benefit you in the end. I'm not talking about walking away from a discussion only to come back later to acquiesce to a supplier's lowest price. The true walkaway is just that—a walkaway.

Some years ago I had been dealing with a pearl farmer in China for nearly a year. Negotiations were fierce each time I visited his factory. We would start early and negotiate all day. He and his colleagues always prolonged the process by taking numerous breaks, going for long lunches, and by taking me out on the town, hoping I would become intoxicated enough to relent to their demands. I didn't like having to draw out the negotiation process because it meant more time away from my business, my family, and my home. But I put up with it because I knew that they produced the best pearls. And they knew that I had no choice but to pay premium prices. Although I always left fairly satisfied with the prices I paid, I didn't like the games, and I wanted to gain the upper hand.

So, one particular time I made a trip there, I tried a different tactic. I contacted the factory and I let the "big boss" know that I was going to be flying back to his city to make a large pearl purchase. When I got there, there were pearls piled high on the table and the boss began telling me what prices he expected. I looked over the pearls and told them that although the pearls were good, and they were exactly what I needed, I was unwilling to pay the prices they demanded. This is when the negotiation game is supposed to begin because they predicted what I would say, and after a few days of negotiation, they were expecting me to agree to their prices—I had always done so in the past, and they knew that I needed the pearls. However, I secretly didn't need any pearls (at that time), so I politely told them "no, thank you," and I left and returned to the United States without buying any pearls at all.

The moral of this story is that negotiation is a game. You can either play their game, or they can play yours. Yes, I invested the time and money going there, but I benefited in the end. When I got back to the United States, I was besieged with e-mails, telephone calls, and faxes. They were offering me deals on all sizes with prices I had never thought possible with this supplier. Now they were after me. This incident let that pearl supplier know that I didn't have to rely on them as a source—walking away sent the message that I could and would find pearls elsewhere. I had them hooked for life.

Now negotiations with this factory take less than an afternoon. They have a new respect for me that I would never have attained if I didn't give them that true walkaway years ago. I've established a long-standing business friendship with this factory. Remember that in business, desperation is expensive, and tenacity means standing your ground.

What Kind of Products to Avoid

There isn't a general rule as to what you can and cannot sell online. Of course, anything you sell must be in compliance with the law. Smaller items are the easiest because they are easy to ship and you don't have to deal with complicated freight charges that go along with shipping bigger items. Selling delicate products that are easily damaged can be challenging because no matter how carefully you pack something, there is a larger risk of damage. Perishable items are also challenging since they require specialized packaging. Try to avoid products with a short market shelf life. They might be hot for a while, but there is no longevity, and if you've bought too much inventory, then you have dead inventory on your hands.

Avoid Fads and Trends (Unless You Are Savvy Enough to be Ahead of the Curve)

Every year a product hits the market like a shooting star. The product is really hot for a couple of seasons or a couple of years, then the product's popularity wanes. This is true of Beanie Babies, pet rocks, pogs, and many other product trends and fads. If you want to be in business for the long haul, then you need to choose a product that has some longevity. Products with a short shelf life can mean disaster for your business, especially if that particular product is the only item you are selling. However, if you are aware of the trend or fad early enough, you can utilize that knowledge to your advantage—just make sure to know when to get out. Otherwise, you will be stuck with tons of worthless inventory.

Stick to products that have proven their staying power, such as jewelry, books, clothing, accessories, etc. But remember, these items typically sell according to brand name as well as market demand and economic considerations. It is crucial to stay ahead of the game and remain aware of the hottest designers and be able to shift quickly with the trends.

1. **Do you like the person you are dealing with?**

   If your instincts tell you that they can't be trusted, then look for another supplier.

2. **How does the new vendor compare with your old vendor?**

   It is very important to compare apples to apples in this scenario. Is this vendor similar to your old one? What can this new vendor do for you that your old vendor was not able to?

3. **Will the new supplier be able to consistently meet the quality and quantity requirements?**

   Your new vendor should be able to keep up with the growth of your business.

4. **How reliable and honest are they?**

   It is important to research the record of a new supplier. Honest and reliable suppliers will always be able to give you references of satisfied customers.

5. **Does the vendor seem too eager to make the sale?**

   If the supplier is too eager to supply you and is willing to offer you an unreasonably low price for the merchandise, remember that if something seems too good to be true, it probably is. Suppliers desperate to make a sale will make loads of empty promises, and you might end up on the losing end.

6. **Is the vendor interested in future sales or is the vendor a "one-trick pony?"**

   If a vendor is interested in a long-term relationship with your business, it is a good indication that they will ship on time, give you fair prices, and establish a working relationship with you conducive to the changing needs of your business.

Finding a Place in the Online World

Finding your product niche is another part of the discovery process in having an online business. The brick-and-mortar world might be oversaturated with certain products, but the online world is different. If people can find a trustworthy and reputable retail site to buy what they need, they will opt for convenience. Try to start small by concentrating on a particular aspect of the market. If you're interested in selling toys, try to hone your product to a particular market of the toy industry. Make sure that you've done your research about the market, the product, and the available suppliers. And most of all develop a true passion for your product.

04

Getting Started

This chapter will give you an overview of the various permits and licenses you will need to obtain; list the various business legal structures that are available to you, and their pros and cons; indicate the importance of a business and financial plan; and take you through the steps of registering your domain name.

Your Business/Domain Name

The first thing to consider is your business name, or username, if selling on a shared venue site. It should reflect what your business is about. When thinking about an appropriate name, try brainstorming and getting input from your friends and family about the name(s) that you're considering. Choose a name that will stick in people's minds, but try not to be too generic. When I began my business, I knew that many potential buyers tend to cruise the Net by typing in a search word. Since I sold pearls, I came up with PearlParadise .com. Thus, I had a name that could be identified with the business, but the word "paradise" connoted something exotic.

Online businesses also have domain names, which is your website address. If you are doing business as "XYXCraftsupply.com," then "XYXCraftsupply .com" is your domain name. Most domain names end in ".com," but other domain names can also end in ".net," ".us," ".info," and ".by." These domain names are not as common, but if the .com name of your choice is taken, you might try the alternatives. The problem with new domain names that use .biz and .info is that users are not as familiar with them, so if the domain name of your choice is PaperSolutions.com and it is taken, you might want to think of another name for your business.

Unlike brick-and-mortar businesses that have an actual location, online retail stores have a virtual physicality that relies heavily on name recognition. So your domain name is everything in online retail. Domain names are the customers' point of destination. If you market your business well, and your business begins to grow and flourish, your domain name is what your customers will associate with. Lose your domain name, and you lose your business. Do not let someone show up three years down the road with papers that prove they had the name first.

Remember to check if a particular domain name is taken, and remember to register and trademark your domain name. Check with the registrar's office and check online to make sure that the name isn't already taken. Sole proprietors doing business under another name will need to register the name with the county, as required by the Trade Name Registration Act.

Also check the trademark status of the name. If you have a logo for your business, you can apply for a trademark registration with the national registry. For more information on trademarks, go to www.uspto.gov. If you're a sole proprietor or a partnership, check with the local county office to make sure that the name isn't already taken. If you're a corporation, check with your state office.

Business Licenses

There are various licenses and permits you need to acquire when starting a business. A business license basically allows you to operate a business. And depending on the nature of your business, you might need more than one. To check your state's requirement, you can log on to www.sba.gov/hotlist/license.html to get a state-by-state listing of the regulations. The following is a list of the various licenses your business might need:

Local Business License: A business license allows you to operate a business within a city jurisdiction. You will need to contact your local city hall or county government offices and inquire about the necessary paperwork and fees involved.

State Business License: A state business license is required if you are selling products or services regulated by state law. You can contact your local government offices to inquire if your business needs a state license.

Federal License: Businesses selling government-regulated products such as alcohol, tobacco, meat, and firearms will need to apply for a federal license. You should consult with an attorney if you feel that you need to apply for a federal license because such businesses tend to have certain liabilities.

Make sure that you understand the requirements for your type of business. These licenses often need to be renewed every few years.

Business Permits

A business permit is required for businesses that buy items from a wholesaler for resale. If you are selling a product online for resale (which means that you will be charging tax for it), then you will need to obtain a seller's permit. A seller's permit is a document that allows you buy wholesale. You can check your local state's requirements by logging on to www.businessnameusa.com. There are various names for a business permit.

- Seller's Permit
- Resale Number
- Reseller License
- Reseller's Tax ID
- Tax Resale ID
- Resale Certificate
- State Tax Resale ID

It might seem confusing, but they are all the same, and acquiring a business permit means that you can buy wholesale (you do not pay tax on your purchases) and sell retail. Home-based online businesses are also required to have a Home Occupation Permit. A Home Occupation Permit allows you to do business in your home and is different from a seller's permit and a business permit. The permit is subject to a filing and may be obtained (depending on your state or city of residence) through the city. In some areas there is a flat fee involved, or you may be charged a percentage of your annual receipts. You will need to contact your local City Hall to inquire about the requirements for your city. For a list of guidelines regarding a home occupation permit, you can log on to www.sba.gov to find out more about permits.

Don't Let This Happen to You

In 2004 I was still at my home office in West Los Angeles, California, but I had a mailbox in Santa Monica because my website listed a Santa Monica mailbox address. One thing you should know about having an online business is that you will not want to list your home address on a website where thousands of people will have access to your domain. This is for your own protection. So, I secured a mailbox address in the nearby city of Santa Monica.

One day I received a letter from the Santa Monica registrar's office. The letter stated that I had a business in Santa Monica, but they didn't have me on their records. They claimed that I needed a business license from the city of Santa Monica. All I had was a PO Box, but the Santa Monica registrar's office fined me $3,000 for doing business over several years and not having a business license in their city.

I always thought that being in online retail meant that I didn't have to deal with the trivialities of obtaining a business license at a particular city because my business wasn't tied to any one location. I never thought about the technicalities of listing an address different from my home office which meant that, technically, I was doing business in Santa Monica, even though all I did there was pick up my mail.

The Lesson Learned:
Know the local rules and regulations of your city to make sure that you're in compliance. Remember that the physical location you publish on your website is, for all intents and purposes, your official physical address.

Tax Identification Number

All businesses need to obtain a Federal Tax Identification Number. This is also known as EIN (Employer Identification Number). Think of it as a Social Security Number for your business. Obtain IRS Form SS-4 for filing. You will need to acquire an EIN when you first start your business. Some states require a state Tax Identification Number, so check with your local state office. Sole proprietorships and partnerships electing to change their business structure will need to apply for a new EIN.

Taxes are inescapable, and failing to file for an EIN can impede the success of your business. Your business might start out small, but if you're serious about having a successful home-based online retail business, you will want to comply with all federal and state tax requirements. To obtain a Tax ID number, contact your local IRS office or call (800) 829-4933.

Business Structure

One of the first things to consider in having a home-based online business is the legal structure of your business. You will need to bear in mind how you want to manage and operate your business. Do you want sole control of the business? Will you have a partner? Do you want your assets protected from potential lawsuits? You can research the pros and cons of all the various business structures by going online, calling your local Chamber of Commerce, going to the public library, or my favorite, calling your local SBA (Small Business Administration) representative and asking questions that pertain exclusively to your type of business. Combining online and offline research is a good way to go because you can ask your local SBA representative questions that pertain only to your type of business. You can also call your local chamber of commerce or go to your local public library. A business structure will determine your level of responsibility and liability. It will also affect your record-keeping system and how much you will need to pay in taxes.

The following are the most common types of business structure:

- *Sole Proprietorship:* Sole proprietorships are the simplest form of business because they allow the owner to keep total control, but there is the risk of endangering personal assets in the event of a lawsuit.
- *Partnership (General Partnership, Limited Partnership, and Silent Partnership):* Partnerships are good for people who want to combine their capital and share business responsibilities.

- *Corporation (also known as a C Corporation):* Corporations seem complicated, but there the business is considered a separate entity and personal assets are protected.

Less common but also possible are the following:

- *LLC (Limited Liability Company):* Limited Liability Companies are gaining popularity because they are less complicated than corporations, and they also protect personal assets.
- *S Corporations:* An S Corporation begins its existence as a general, for-profit corporation upon filing the Articles of Incorporation at the state level.

Legal Structure Considerations

When choosing the legal structure best suited to fit your needs and your situation, consider these three main points:

- Liability: your duty or obligation to another party based on a written or oral agreement
- Taxes: Money you will owe the government from the course of doing business
- Ownership: the state of owning something (property, business, idea)

Sole Proprietorship

Most small-business owners begin as sole proprietors. A sole proprietorship legally recognizes you and the business as a single entity, which means that you are singularly responsible for liabilities that you may incur in the process of doing business. You should keep your business and personal expenses separate by keeping a separate bank account for your business. Keep accurate records of your expenditures. You might want to do your own bookkeeping or hire an accountant. Nevertheless, when you start your business, you will be starting small, but keep in mind that you are in this for the long haul and you must always think about your business growth. You will need to acquire the appropriate business license(s) and seller's permit as a sole proprietor, but this structure is the least complicated of all business structures.

Sole proprietors file their business income tax on their personal income tax return, which means that your business earnings and any other earnings you make are taxed together. The IRS refers to this system as "pass-through" taxation—your business profits are taxed along with your other earnings, but you are taxed only once. You will file a 1040 form along with a Schedule C (profit and loss from a business) when you file your tax returns. Remember that you should consider setting aside a percentage of your income throughout the year since no one will be deducting taxes on what you've earned. This will help you avoid getting hit with a huge debt to the taxman when April 15 rolls around.

If you're married and your spouse helps out in the business or has participated in the start-up cost of the business, you can still maintain the business as a sole proprietorship. You have the option of either filing a joint Schedule C or filing separately.

Pros
- The most common and simplest business structure.
- You can maintain total control of the business.
- Simple tax filings.

Cons
- You are financially responsible for all business expenses and your assets are not protected.
- A spouse's personal assets are endangered in the event of a business liability or a lawsuit.
- Difficult to raise capital.

General Partnership

This form of legal structure constitutes two or more individuals sharing the profit and loss of a business, any business-related decision making, and the various responsibilities that ensue in the operation and management of a business. If you are interested in forming a business partnership, one of the issues you would have to consider is the nature of your relationship with your potential partner.

- Can you work with this person?
- Is this a person you can trust?
- What is this person's work ethic?
- How much capital can the potential partner contribute?

A business partnership for a home-based online retail business is the same in the brick-and-mortar world. Business partnerships are usually formed for the following reasons:

- Two or more individuals have developed a business idea or have co-invented a product that they want to sell.
- One individual does not have enough capital to start a business.
- The business is a combination of two unique skill sets.

Business partners share in the profits of a business as well as the managerial and business decisions. In the brick-and-mortar world, partners might work out of the same office or storefront, but for a home-based online business, partners have the option of working in their own homes, or they can choose which partner's house the main business will be located in. There should also be a clarification between partners as to where inventory is kept and a detailed listing of each partner's business responsibilities. These items can be delineated in the partnership agreement. Although the basis of a partnership is that the partners have an equal say in the decision-making of a business, everything will depend on the dynamics between the partners involved. The following are the characteristics of a general partnership:

- There is a verbal or written agreement between partners.
- There must be an existing business. This can be done by registering the business.
- Partners share in the rights, interests, and goals of the business.
- Partners must engage in a for-profit venture. Nonprofit organizations cannot be partnerships.

Partnerships can be formed with just a verbal agreement between interested parties, but it is advisable to have a written document of the agreement delineating the respective partners' responsibility and financial input. Such a document serves to clarify the function of each partner and it can help prevent possible future misunderstandings between the partners.

Proceed with Caution

Be sure to draft a partnership agreement when entering into a partnership.

It is also important that you understand the elements that would constitute a partner. If another party puts up the capital to start your business, that person does not necessarily have to be a partner. A business partner is characterized by the following:

- Joint ownership: Both parties have a vested interest and thus share in the profit and loss of the business.
- Participation in gross returns: Partners must share in the gross returns of the business, and the share is commensurate to the partner's financial investment.
- Sharing of profits: Sharing of profits would constitute a partnership agreement.
- Sharing of losses: The parties involved share in the losses of a business.

A business partnership has its advantages and disadvantages. Entering into such an agreement with another individual is almost like a marriage. And the dynamics between the parties involved can change depending on the climate of each individual's ability to become involved in the business. Unlike a sole proprietorship, you share the responsibilities of the business and share in the good and bad times.

Pros
- Sharing in the responsibilities of a business can alleviate the pressure of having to do it alone.
- Partners can share in the financial responsibilities of the start-up cost and everyday business expenses.
- A partner can provide moral and emotional support.
- Partners can designate responsibilities according to each partner's strengths and weaknesses.
- There is no double taxation. As with sole proprietorship, partners can benefit from pass-through taxation.

Cons

- There are often misunderstandings between partners.
- Conflict in financial and business management can ensue.
- If one partner becomes insolvent, the other solvent partner(s) will have to be responsible for any loss or liability incurred.
- Solvent partners can have unlimited personal liability.

Don't Jump in Headfirst

Know your potential partner! A key piece of advice from Ryan Totka of Tornado Promotions.com is to perform a background check on potential partners.

Limited Partnership

Limited partnerships are usually formed to raise capital. This type of business structure constitutes a general partner and a limited partner. A general partner can have unlimited liability, but a limited partner's liability is dependent on his financial investment in the company. In a limited partnership the limited partner must file taxes as a separate entity from the business.

Limited Partnerships

In a limited partnership, each partner has a limited liability—the partners are only liable for the amount that is commensurate to the amount of their registered investment. For example, if a partnership is found liable for a $100,000 debt, and a limited partner in that business invested $10,000, the limited partner is only liable for the amount of his/her investment. Limited partners usually have no authority over the management of the business.

Pros

- A limited partner's liability is commensurate to his/her investment.
- A limited partner has less involvement (this is good if the limited partner trusts and generally agrees with the general partner's business decisions).

Cons

- A limited partner has less control and/or power over business decisions.

Silent Partnership

In some cases partnerships are formed with a silent partner. A silent partner (sleeping partner) is not involved in the decision-making aspect of the business but still shares in the profits and losses of a business. This partner's involvement with the business is not normally publicly known. The silent partner usually provides needed capital in the business that the general partners are not financially able to provide.

Pros

- Silent partners usually do not involve themselves in the daily management and operations of the business.

Cons

- A silent partner's lack of involvement in a business can sometimes create friction in the sharing of profits, especially with partners who are actively involved in the business.

Main Points in a Partnership Agreement

- Delineate Amount of Investment by Each Partner
- Delineate Sharing of Profits
- Delineate Sharing of Losses
- Itemize Sharing of Labor/Responsibilities
- Delineate Skills of Each Partner
- Delineate Terms of Dissolution of Business Partnership

C Corporation

Although most home-based online businesses start out as sole proprietorships or partnerships, a time will come when the individuals involved will consider incorporating their business. The term for changing a particular business structure into a corporation is referred to as "incorporation." The most common type of corporation is referred to as a C Corporation (a standard business corporation). It is advisable that you consult a lawyer when deciding to incorporate, but researching the matter for yourself can save you money. You can file incorporations yourself though sites such as www.bizfilings .com. A corporation is recognized as a separate entity from the individual(s) involved in the business. Incorporating your business requires that you file Articles of Incorporation or a Certificate of Incorporation to your state office. You will need to pay a filing fee, and you can check your state's website for specific fees and regulations. A couple of factors to think about when deciding whether to incorporate are the following:

- Protection of personal assets
- Raising capital
- Possible loss of control in the decision-making aspect of the business. This means that you no longer have the power to make decisions in the business. For example, if you believe that your online business needs to make a $50,000 investment in print advertising, you will no longer have the power to make such decisions on your own unless the issue has been discussed and approved by the appropriate individuals of the corporation.

The corporate structure is comprised of shareholders, directors, and officers. To complete the incorporation, you must conduct an organizational meeting to adopt the bylaws and to distribute the certificates for shareholders after Articles of Incorporation are filed. The corporate secretary should keep minutes of the meeting, and Articles of Incorporation and meeting minutes should be kept in a safe place.

Although shareholders don't make management decisions, they have the power to elect and remove directors, vote on corporate issues, and approve or disapprove amendments. Directors have the power to appoint officers of the corporation and make management decisions. Officers, who usually make daily business decisions, are appointed by the board of directors. In some cases an individual can become a corporation, with said individual occupying the role of shareholder, director, and officer. It is advisable to consult an attorney or accountant if you are unclear about the benefits of incorporation for your business.

Pros

- No personal liability.
- Ownership is easily transferred.
- Capital can be raised through sale of stocks.
- Established credibility.
- Retirement plans easily established.

Cons

- Complex formation.
- More expensive to incorporate.
- Double taxation.
- Extensive record keeping.

Pass-Through Taxation

The income of the corporation is passed on to the individual shareholders and/or members of the corporation. There is no double taxation in S Corporations.

S Corporation

An S Corporation is like a C Corporation—they are both legal entities that require the filing of Articles of Incorporation. The main difference is that an S Corporation can enjoy pass-through taxation by filing Form 2553 with the IRS. To qualify for S Corporation status, the corporation must have between 1 and 100 shareholders. The following is a list of requirements for S Corporation status:

- Corporation can only have between 1 and 100 shareholders.
- Corporation must be within the United States.
- Shareholders must be US citizens or resident aliens.
- Only one class of stock can be issued.
- Shareholders must unanimously agree to elect S Corporation status.
- Company must elect to change corporate status within the time frame required.
- Some banks, insurance companies, DISCs (domestic international sales corporations), and possession corporations (corporations under US possessions such as Puerto Rico) are not qualified for S Corporation status.

Pros

- Pass-through taxation.

Cons

- Limits the number of shareholders.
- Corporation cannot be in another country.
- Shareholders must be US citizens or resident aliens.
- Change of corporate status is within a time frame.

Where to Incorporate

If you will be doing business primarily in your home state, then it is wise to incorporate your business there. However, if you do business in other states, then your business can qualify as a "foreign corporation," which means that you can incorporate in another state. The state of choice is usually Delaware because:

- Delaware has one of the lowest incorporation fees in the country.
- In the event of a lawsuit, Delaware does not use juries, but appointed judges who deal specifically with corporate law.
- An individual can hold all the officer positions.
- Corporate shareholders, directors, and officers do not have to be Delaware residents.
- Stock shares held by non-Delaware residents are not subject to Delaware state taxes.
- Businesses that are incorporated in Delaware, but that reside outside Delaware, are not subject to corporate income tax.

Interesting Facts

- S Corporations and LLCs are gaining popularity over the more traditional C Corporations.
- More than 50 percent of Fortune 500 companies are incorporated in Delaware.

Requirements	Sole Proprietorship	General Partnership	C Corporation	S Corporation	Limited Liability Company (LLC)
State filing and fees	No state filing. No State filing fee.	No state filing. No State filing fee.	Requires state filing. Verbal or written agreement between parties.	Requires state filing of Articles of Incorporation and state filing fees.	Requires state filing of Articles of Incorporation and state filing fees.
Taxation requirements	Pass-through taxation. Sole owner pays all taxes.	Pass-through taxation. Partners pay their own tax.	Double taxation. Taxed at entity level and on distributed dividends to shareholders.	Pass-through taxation.	Pass-through taxation.
Liability	Owner has unlimited liability.	Partners have unlimited liability.	Shareholders are not usually liable for debts of corporation.	Shareholders are not usually liable for debts of corporation.	Members are not usually liable for debts of LLC.
Capital	Capital raised by sole proprietor.	Partners must be responsible for raising capital.	Stock can be sold to raise capital.	Stock can be sold to raise capital.	Interest can be sold to raise capital depending on operating agreement.

Limited Liability Company (LLC)

Although fairly new, more small-business owners are choosing to become Limited Liability Companies. The LLC can be described as a fusion between a corporation and a partnership. LLCs require a state filing, as with S and C Corporations. LLCs offer the same liability protection, but LLC owners aren't subjected to double taxation. Banks, nonprofit organizations, and insurance companies cannot qualify for LLC status. An LLC can have an unlimited number of members, but it can also be a "single-member" LLC. Unlike corporations, LLCs are not required to have annual meetings. People are not as familiar with LLCs, but they do have their advantages and disadvantages. LLCs are gaining popularity because they offer the benefits of corporations and the less complex operational structure of partnerships.

Pros

- Less complicated than a C or S Corporation.
- Pass-through taxation.
- Unlimited number of members.
- Limited personal liability for owners.

Cons

- Requires state filing and fees.
- More paperwork than a partnership.
- A dissolution date may be required in some states.

Writing a Successful Business Plan

Some might think that having to write a business plan to start a home-based online business is too complicated. A background in business is not necessary to devise a business plan, and if you have a working knowledge of the fundamental categories of a business plan, it is not difficult. Having a business plan will help you get started in forming the concept, strategy, and financing of your business, and it will also help you with expanding your business.

A business plan is a written document delineating your company's management and financial strategy for a given period of time. It should convince potential investors and partners that your business is worth the investment. (See pages 63–65 for a sample business plan.) The questions you should be prepared to answer are:

- How do you plan to run your business?
- What are your short-term and long-term goals?
- How are you going to achieve those goals?
- Who is going to buy your product?
- How do you plan to market it?

Developing a business plan will help you look at your ideas and product more objectively. You will have to do some research on the market demand for your product as well as management strategies. This will help you develop your thoughts and ideas about the market potential for your product and the upcoming changes in market and product niche. It can also help you adapt your business to the fluctuations of the market and your personal life.

In addition, if you plan to finance your business yourself, you can avoid costly management mistakes by having a written idea of your business objectives and strategies. A business plan can also help you get the financing you need if you don't have the start-up capital. If you apply for a bank loan, banks will require that you have a business plan. There are services and software that can help you in developing one, but it's important that you know the basics.

Since a large percentage of businesses (either online or brick-and-mortar) fail every year, a written plan can help the new business owner survive the ups and downs. Part of your success in the online world is being well prepared before you even make your first sale—you do not want your business to be a casualty of poor planning. Think of a business plan as your reference. A well-written business plan should detail the concept and strategy of your business, and it is something that you can refer to now and again. It might also undergo changes through time. It is a good idea to update your business plan in the event that the business needs financing. A business plan will generally have the following categories: executive summary, company summary (overview), product summary, market summary and strategy, management summary, and financial summary. These categories will define your business, and they will help you in the long run to effectively manage your business.

Executive Summary

A summary of the various sections of the business plan. Since this is the first document a future lender will read, it should be a persuasive statement that showcases the strength and potential of your business.

Company Summary

This section should specify the vision of the company, its business structure, and projected evolution in a given period of time. If the company is new, then a summary of personnel or the company's unique product niche should be mentioned.

> "Be ready to evolve and change your business model, as things change (as they always will). Don't get stuck with your head in the mud or sand, especially since most of us need shared selling venues, and they are always changing the guidelines, so you must be ready to adjust accordingly. And don't grumble—it only drags down your business and your mental outlook and doesn't help you grow. Don't forget to have fun!"
>
> —*Bob Willey, Owner,* Bob's Neat Stuff and Bob's Neat Books, http://bobsstuff.com, http://bobsneatbooks.com

Product Summary

A summary detailing the product you wish to sell, its niche in the market, and its prices in comparison to the competition. This section may mention product history, if it is a product in development or if it's already in the market. Indicate if the product is manufactured by the business.

Market Summary and Strategy

A summary of your target market, focusing specifically on demographics and whether your price points are in alignment with what the target market is willing to pay for. This summary should also delineate the market history of your product and its current standing in the market. Include the strengths and weaknesses of the competition and how your business plans to capitalize on this issue. A list of innovative marketing strategies will make this section attractive to investors and lenders.

Management Summary

This section serves as a detailed summary of your management team. Think of it as a resume of the qualifications and work history of the people involved in the business, their function in the business, education background, and their planned salaries and benefits.

Financial Summary

This section summarizes the accounting system of your business, how much capital you have or will need, and the financial projection of running your business. Those seeking financing will need to provide the potential investor or lender with a financial forecast (an assumption of the company's cash inflow and outflow).

Business plans can vary depending on the length and nature of your business. Certain sections, such as the management summary, may be included in the company summary if the company is just beginning. Writing a business plan can also be a process of discovery. You might find out that you have to reevaluate some of your original ideas because your research has provided you with new information, or you might want to rethink your company's structure; nevertheless, remember that a business plan serves as a template for your business before you even get started, and when things get chaotic you can revert

Company Summary

ABCRarebooks.com is an online retail bookstore that specializes in rare and out-of-print books. The company is currently a single proprietorship, but it is projected to become an S Corporation in twelve months. My vision for ABCRarebooks.com is to satisfy the needs of scholars and book collectors who want to obtain rare and out-of-print books. The target customer currently only has access to rare and out-of-print books in specialty bookstores that are located in metropolitan areas of the United States. Although there are small bookstores that deal with rare and out-of-print books in some small towns, their "out-of-the-way" location makes it hard for the target customers to easily access the products they have to offer. As an online bookstore, ABCRarebooks.com aims to reach collectors from all over the world. I position ABCRarebooks.com to be a leading seller of rare and out-of-print books that offers a ninety-day guarantee of the product.

As the sole proprietor of this online bookstore, I have twenty years of experience as a bookseller and trader in the Los Angeles area. I have dealt with collectors from all over the world who travel the globe to buy specialty books. I understand the market demand and product availability of my merchandise.

Product Summary

Rare and out-of-print books are an unknown commodity in the book market. There are brick-and-mortar bookstores offering these types of books, but their selection is limited and their prices are high because of the high overhead of the brick-and-mortar retail business. The quality of the books is also not very good. The books that ABCRarebooks.com will offer are in mint condition. I source the books from estate sales and through my association with various booksellers and traders all over the United States and Europe.

The books sold at ABCRarebooks.com will be 40–50 percent off their market price due to the low overhead of e-retail and because I buy directly from the source. The books available at my site will deal in various genres of rare and out-of-print fiction and nonfiction books. Part of the inventory will also be autographed by the writers of the books. This is a rather rare occurrence in the specialty book market, but my online store will have 50 percent of this type of merchandise.

Market Summary

The target market consists primarily of book collectors and scholars. Most have a bachelor's degree or higher, and they are usually educators, artists, and writers. The income range of my target customers is between $75,000 and $250,000. In the brick-and-mortar world, these books are usually priced between $100 and $5,000 (depending on the book), but ABCRarebooks.com will sell the product at 50 percent off its market price. My product will also be made available to other booksellers and traders.

Despite the small market for rare and out-of-print books, the target customers have always pursued this commodity, and the popularity and demand for out-of-print books is growing.

Our competition will mainly be online booksellers and offline bookstores dealing in the same product. Offline bookstores have higher prices, and their location makes it difficult for buyers out of their geographical area to reach them. Their high overhead also compels them to sell the books at a high price point. Online booksellers have a low overhead, but most of these owners do not have my experience, and they usually source through a middleman. They might be entrepreneurs, but I have the entrepreneurial instinct and experience, which sets me above the competition.

My marketing strategy for my business will consist of press releases, seminars, trade shows, and testimonials on my website from various clients I have dealt with in the past. I will offer numerous related articles on my website to showcase my expertise in the subject. I will also optimize my website and implement the necessary security measures to gain customer trust. Because I am also a photographer, I plan to take detailed pictures of my merchandise and provide very specific descriptions about the condition of the book, its history, and its value in the market. I will provide price comparisons so that my customers will have an idea of how much they can save by buying from my website. I will also offer frequent customer discounts, and I will offer my loyal customers promotions on specially selected books that are available exclusively to them. I plan to advertise in trade magazines and journals, and I plan to conduct seminars about the subject to attract attention to my website.

Management Summary

As the sole owner of the business, I will handle all aspects of the business for the next twelve months. I have twenty years of experience in managing a specialty bookstore that deals with rare and out-of-print books. I attended Pepperdine University and earned my doctorate in English literature. I have been involved in selling, evaluating, and appraising rare and out-of-print books since I graduated from college. I managed a specialty bookstore for twenty years, and the contacts that I have made have proven to be a valuable asset in my online business. My main function in the business is to buy inventory, appraise the quality and value of the books, photograph the products, and write the product description of the books that I offer for sale on my website. I will also track my sales, keep the accounting, and ship the merchandise. Because I have enough savings to sustain the business and to meet my personal financial obligations for the next six months, I will draw a salary after the first six months of business.

Financial Summary

My initial investment in the business will be $10,000, and I will use a space in my home as an office. I plan to finance the purchase of a new computer and any other necessary start-up expenses by using my credit card. I will finance the business with my savings and with the additional income that I receive in my work as a consultant for various bookstores that are looking to change the make-up of their inventory. I plan to keep the accounting using the software program QuickBooks.

back to this document to help you get back on track. Even more important is the audience of this business plan. If you're seeking financing, remember that your business plan should convince and persuade the reader that your business is, indeed, worth the investment.

Sound Financial Planning

The acquisition, management, and investment of money are fundamental at the start of any business. Think of it this way: A business is similar to an automobile because money in business is what gas is to a car. A car won't start without gas, and a business cannot get started without capital. A sound financial plan will help your business get started, and the various financial projections you make will let you know how to manage and utilize your funds. A financial plan is different from a business plan in that a financial plan delineates your capital and spending strategy for the business, whereas a business plan delineates the decision-making aspect within the business. Creating a financial plan for your business is important, especially if you plan to seek financing. Banks and investors want to see that you have thoroughly planned the course of your financial actions because it not only indicates that you've done your research, it also lets them know that your business is a lucrative investment. Although most small businesses tend to self-finance, you should create a financial plan to help you determine your current financial standings, as well as to help determine how your business will grow in the near future. Having a business involves money. So ask yourself the following questions:

- How do I plan to get the capital to start my business?
- Will I self-finance, borrow from relatives and/or friends, or go to a bank?
- Will I keep or quit my job?

Most home-based online businesses are initially begun with the owner working on the business on a part-time basis. I stayed with the airlines for a couple of years so that I could afford to work full time on my business. Consider the advantages of staying in your current job to retain medical and dental benefits for you and/or your family. Regardless of which route you plan to take, assessing your situation will help you in writing your financial plan, and it will help you understand how much money you need to begin and how much money you will need to run your business before you see profit.

The first thing you will need to do is take inventory of your assets, income, and current expenses. How much money do you have left each month after all the bills have been paid? Do you have savings that you want to invest in your business? Do you plan to take a cash advance on a credit card (be careful of this because of interest)? The following are the various options for a business owner to obtain capital:

- Personal savings
- Banks and credit union
- Relatives and friends
- Home equity loans
- Partnering
- Credit cards
- Accounts receivable financing
- Purchase order financing
- Employee stock ownership

Once you determine your current financial standing and how you will get capital for your business, set a goal for your business and project future expenditures.

- What is your realistic projected timeline for realizing a profit?
- What is your initial start-up cost?
- How much money do you need to pay for monthly projected expenses?
- How much do you need to sell to cover expenses over the next three to six months?

Then determine a strategic course of action:

- How will you get there?
- What are your plans to achieve your goals?

Now, begin to take inventory of your projected initial start-up costs and expenses. Start-up costs are the expenses you will make to get your business started, such as filing fees, website design, and office equipment. Expenses can be put into two categories: fixed expenses and variables. Fixed expenses are continuous but are not subject to change. Variables are your monthly recurring expenses that might or might not fluctuate in a given period of time, such as inventory, shipping expenses, merchant fees for credit cards, taxes, and other supplies that you will need to buy from time to time.

Make a list of your initial start-up costs along with fixed and variable expenses. If you are going to make a six-month projection of the capital that you will need, multiply your fixed and variable expenses by six, then add that amount to your initial start-up cost. The total amount will let you know how much capital you need to survive in the next six months without considering sales. You can determine your monthly expenses by dividing your total fixed and variable expenses for the next six months by six. You can add the total of your initial start-up cost to determine your first-month expense. After determining the figures, assess your current financial standing. Can you self-finance over the next six months, or will you need to seek financing elsewhere?

Now that you have these figures, keep in mind the changes in the market and economics, which means eventually your financial plan will also have to change because these circumstances have an effect on your business goal. Keep your plan up-to-date, especially if you plan to seek outside financing in the future.

How to Stay within Your Budget

Once your have a written financial plan, staying within your business budget can be challenging. Unexpected circumstances such as changes in tax laws, changes in the business climate, and changes in income can affect your financial situation. But aside from issues that you can't control, you *can* control your spending habits. Purchasing certain luxuries for your business, such as new office equipment, when your old equipment would suffice is an unnecessary expense, especially if you're working on a shoestring budget. So when the urge to purchase an unnecessary item haunts you, remember that frugality has saved more businesses from going under than extravagance.

Frivolous Expenses for an Online Business

- Fancy letterheads, envelopes, and/or business cards
- Unnecessary inventory
- Office equipment (fancy desk, chair, etc.)
- Outsourcing services that you can do yourself
- Trendy office gadgets

ABCRarebooks.com

FINANCIAL STATEMENT
2011 and 2012

CONTENTS

ABCRarebooks.com

BALANCE SHEETS

2012

ASSETS

	2012	2011
CURRENT ASSETS		
Cash and cash equivalents	$ 669,581	$ 624,716
Investments	3,762,098	3,662,709
Trade accounts receivable	687,882	161,197
Prepaid expenses	86,697	125,592
Other current assets	267,789	128,530
Total Current Assets	5,474,047	4,702,744
PROPERTY AND EQUIPMENT, at cost	1,117,091	858,951
Less accumulated depreciation and amortization	(687,840)	(575,841)
Total Property and Equipment	429,251	283,110
OTHER ASSETS		
Other assets	14,364	14,364
Total Other Assets	14,364	14,364
TOTAL ASSETS	**$ 5,917,662**	**$ 5,000,218**

ABCRarebooks.com

BALANCE SHEETS

December 31, 2012 and 2011

LIABILITIES AND SHAREHOLDERS' EQUITY

	2012	2011
CURRENT LIABILITIES		
Trade accounts payable	$ 76,145	$ 36,754
Accrued expenses	330,127	140,041
Deferred revenue	2,131,138	1,655,796
Total Current Liabilities	2,537,410	1,832,591
COMMITMENTS AND CONTINGENCIES		
SHAREHOLDERS' EQUITY		
Common stock, no par value, 2,000,000 shares authorized, 1,006,500 shares issued and outstanding	11,226	11,145
Retained earnings	3,067,434	2,905,183
Accumulated other comprehensive income	301,592	251,299
Total Shareholders' Equity	3,380,252	3,167,627
TOTAL LIABILITIES AND SHAREHOLDERS' EQUITY	**$5,917,662**	**$5,000,218**

ABCRarebooks.com

STATEMENTS OF INCOME

December 31, 2012 and 2011

	2012	2011
REVENUE		
Software	$ 5,577,717	$ 4,510,820
Technical support	3,306,041	3,135,899
Training	742,446	667,866
User seminars	633,164	487,736
Total Revenue	10,259,368	8,802,321
EXPENSES		
Programming, support, and training	4,499,318	4,077,998
Selling and marketing	1,720,615	1,287,164
General and administrative	2,301,471	1,980,900
Total Expenses	8,521,404	7,346,062
NET INCOME FROM OPERATIONS	1,737,964	1,456,259
OTHER INCOME		
Interest and dividends	83,911	64,238
Net realized investment gains	92,369	23,127
Rental Income	1,885	-0-
Total Other Income	178,165	87,365
NET INCOME	**$1,916,129**	**$1,543,624**

ABCRarebooks.com

STATEMENTS OF CASH FLOWS

December 31, 2012 and 2011

	2012	2011
CASH FLOWS FROM OPERATING ACTIVITIES		
Net income	$ 1,296,106	$ 1,127,661
Adjustments to reconcile net income to net cash provided by operating activities:		
Depreciation and amortization	112,000	76,108
(Increase) decrease in assets:		
Trade accounts receivable	(526,685)	21,364
Other current assets	(139,258)	(91,445)
Prepaid expenses	38,895	(36,620)
Increase (decrease) in liabilities:		
Trade accounts payable	39,391	35,631
Net Cash Provided by Operating Activities	1,485,876	1,382,460
CASH FLOWS FROM INVESTING ACTIVITIES		
Purchase of property and equipment	(258,141)	(87,420)
Net Cash Used in Investing Activities	(258,141)	(87,420)
CASH FLOWS FROM FINANCING ACTIVITIES		
Investments	(49,095)	(356,589)
Sale of options	80	-0-
Dividends paid	(1,133,855)	(677,232)
Net Cash Used in Financing Activities	(1,182,870)	(1,033,821)
NET INCREASE (DECREASE) IN CASH AND CASH EQUIVALENTS	44,865	261,219
CASH AND CASH EQUIVALENTS, BEGINNING OF YEAR	624,716	363,497
CASH AND CASH EQUIVALENTS, END OF YEAR	**$669,581**	**$624,716**
SUPPLEMENTAL DISCLOSURE		
Cash paid during the period for interest	$ -0-	$ -0-

Online and Offline Research

Getting your business started requires a lot of research. You might have a background in business, but saving yourself money means having to obtain certain information for yourself. You might have to make some calls to your local and state offices to find out about business licenses and permits. Or you might want to talk to small-business owners and ask them what it was like getting started. You can scour your local bookstores for further reading about the Internet, marketing, and website design, or you can go to the local library.

Research might take some time, but you're better off in the long run because information is power. The Internet has also become a valuable tool in researching what you need to know. You can search for just about anything online, but make sure that the information you are getting is correct. If you are researching business licenses, look at a couple of sites to check for consistency of information. Research gives you the knowledge of all aspects of your business, even if you don't plan to do it yourself. For instance, it might be a good idea to hire a professional website designer to create your site, but you can establish some control if you have a working knowledge of website design.

Although researching online is fast and convenient, sometimes nothing replaces the human element when it comes to information. Schooling might be considered part of your research, but the important thing to consider is that you don't want to venture into owning a business if you don't know what's going on. The following is a list of websites that might help you get started:

- Small Business Administration: www.sba.gov
- Entrepreneur: www.entrepreneur.com
- Internal Revenue Service: www.irs.gov
- Census Bureau: www.census.gov

Effective Record Keeping

I mentioned in chapter 3 the importance of separating your personal records from your business records. Being organized and having everything in its proper place helps your business run properly and smoothly. Always update files and keep all paperwork in order because that is one way of protecting your business. Corporations should keep a separate file of all corporate meetings and minutes. Having a paper trail of your business effects makes things easier in the event of a tax audit.

More important is that keeping an up-to-date record of accounts payables and receivables also lets you know your business situation. There are various programs such as QuickBooks to help you with accounting, and color coding your files can help you run an efficient online business.

How to Stay Organized

Organization is not that difficult; it's just about putting things in their proper place. Another aspect of organization is deciding how the work should be divided if you are in a partnership, or deciding the function of individuals in a corporation or LLC. You should have a work system in mind when you first begin, but also keep in mind that you might have to amend the system as your business grows. Establish your long-term and short-term priorities, and keep a daily to-do list. Although you have an online business, papers can still pile up. Make effective use of current technology to avoid undue paperwork; this also means that you will have to constantly update your database. Your business might start out small, but the goal is to build up your business, and you want to create a tight management and operating system to ensure success.

I have given you a lot to think about. As you reflect on your choices, remember that having a successful business is having the attitude that you are in this to make money. A successful business requires planning and thought.

When to Know That You Can't Do It All

Most small businesses start as a single individual doing everything, but it won't always be that way. If you do all your research, you will establish a working knowledge of all the business aspects. You might want to hire a service to file your business license and permits, Articles of Incorporation, and EIN numbers—or you might not. Your decision will depend on how much time and money you have to outsource or do it yourself.

Nevertheless, as your business grows you will realize that you won't be able to do everything yourself. Time management is important in terms of prioritizing, but a time will come when you will need to hire employees to assist you. You might need to place an ad or hire a temp agency. Always weigh out your options. If you realize that you are shipping late or not processing incoming orders in a timely manner, then you will need to hire someone else. You have the option of hiring part-time or full-time employees; this decision will depend on the nature of your business and how much you want to spend. You might be a one-person operation now, but it won't always be that way. Your goal is to grow your business, and if things become stagnant because you can't do it all, then it's time to hire someone. I will discuss this further in chapter 13, but the issue of growth is something that you should always keep in mind.

When you start your home-based online business, it is reasonable for you to face certain difficulties and obstacles, but tenacity in achieving your dream will get you through these uncertain times, and if you know what you are getting into by doing your research, you can minimize some unpleasant surprises along the way. I hope that I've taken some of the mystery out of becoming a business owner. There is a gamut of information out there, and all you need to do is know what to look for.

05

Legal and Ethical Issues

We live in a litigious society. Lawsuits are expensive, time-consuming, and most of all they can disrupt the normal flow of a business. Avoiding costly lawsuits is one way a business owner can stay in the black. No doubt you have enough to worry about when starting an online business without getting entangled in a legal knot in the process. One way to avoid the legal pitfalls is to understand that what pertains in the offline world also pertains in the online world—issues such as product liability, trademark infringement, and copyright. Words such as arbitration and litigation should only cross your path in theory and not in practice. In other words, you should always try to avoid legal troubles. An ounce of prevention can mean thousands of dollars saved in attorney's fees.

Moreover, although you might have to seek the advice of a lawyer at some point, taking preventive measures to lessen your legal expenses should be a primary concern. Business owners should take the following attitude (**PEP**): **P**repare for the worst and **E**xpect the worst in order to **P**revent the worst from happening. Remember that every aspect of your business at one time or another will likely be under the scrutiny of the legal system.

Words of Wisdom

"I can't do literary work for the rest of this year because I'm meditating another lawsuit and looking around for a defendant."

—*Mark Twain*

Domain Name

The popularity of online shopping has spawned a gamut of online retailers looking to find success. Can you imagine how crowded the world would be if every domain name had a physical setting in the offline world? Well, the online world has gotten crowded, too, resulting in endless conflicts over domain names. If you think that your idea for a domain name is unique—you'd better think again. As we discussed previously, if you have come up with a domain name that is not registered, then you had better hurry up and register your domain name before it is taken. Companies such as Nike, Reebok, and Louis Vuitton all have brand name recognition, and they protect their names like a tigress protecting her cubs.

Once you register your domain name, you legally own the license to use it so long as the name does not infringe on an already trademarked name or logo. If you have, in good faith, registered a trademarked domain name, you can still continue with your business so long as the company does not contact you. Domain name disputes fall into the following categories:

- Domain Name vs. Domain Name
- Domain Name vs. Trademark Name
- Business Name vs. Trademarked Domain Name
- Domain Name vs. Trademarked Domain Name
- Business Name vs. Name of a Trademarked Product

Domain name disputes can be settled through the following means:

- Agreement between both parties
- Court action
- Arbitration

Upon judgment, the losing party must transfer, suspend, or cancel the domain name of the business. You want to avoid becoming either the defendant or the plaintiff in this situation, so it is best to do the following:

- Register your domain name
- Obtain a trademark registration on your domain name
- Do not use a trademarked domain name

You are in this business to make money, so it is best not to take chances with issues such as domain names because legal issues can disrupt the flow of your business and hiring expensive lawyers can dry up your capital.

Cybersquatting

The practice of registering domain names that contain the name of an already registered trademark, then selling the name to the domain owner at an exorbitant price.

Trademark

Trademark disputes occur when two companies selling the same or similar products have the same domain name or logo. One party usually owns the trademark and the other is using the name without the authorization or knowledge of the trademark owner. Some businesses think that they can get the advantage of name recognition if their domain name is identifiable with a recognized brand, but it is only a matter of time before someone catches on. It doesn't work in your favor, anyway. You might poach some of your competitor's customers, but you're not creating your own solid customer base, either. Ultimately, you're just confusing potential customers. If you have designed a trademark for your business, it is wise to obtain a trademark registration to protect yourself from those attempting to capitalize on the success of your domain name or product logo.

If you have ownership of a trademark and someone else is using it as a domain name or logo, you can log on to www.ustpo.gov for more information about taking action and filing a complaint. You can search the USPTO database to find out if a domain name has been trademarked. If the name or logo has not been trademarked, you will need to fill out a trademark application along with a written description of the goods (applications cannot be completed without a product description).

Copyright Infringement

Copyright infringement is the unauthorized use of copyrighted audio, visual, or written text. Stealing someone else's stuff, even if it's a slogan and not a diamond ring, is considered theft, and legal actions can be taken against you. Blatant copyright infringement occurs in the brick-and-mortar world all the time—all you have to do is walk a big-city street and you will see individuals selling bootleg copies of music and movies. Instances of copyright infringement in the online retail world include the selling of bootleg copies of CDs, DVDs, and/or written material, such as: musical works, literary works, graphics, and artwork. Violation of copyright is a strict liability tort (crime), which means that the plaintiff only needs to prove that the defendant committed the violation. There are no excuses of good faith acts in copyright infringement.

Product Liability

As a retailer, you have the responsibility of delivering to the buyer quality merchandise that lives up to your advertising claim of the product. If a buyer receives merchandise that is defective, or if the merchandise causes injury, the buyer has the legal right to pursue a product liability claim against your business. Although product liability laws vary from state to state, the premise of the law is to protect the consumer from receiving defective or harmful merchandise from the seller, and to prevent or discourage the manufacturer, distributor, or retailer from selling potentially harmful or defective merchandise to the consumer. Product liability laws cover the following issues:

Negligence

The seller is considered negligent if the seller does not warn customers of product defect, manufacturing defect, or potential defect.

Breach of Warranty

Manufacturers or sellers who break a promise regarding the state of the product, or whose product is not as described, are held responsible for breaking the warranty of a product. In online retail the most common reason for a breach of warranty is the claim the product purchased is not what the buyer expected.

Noncompliance of Consumer Protection Act

Sellers who do not disclose certain information about a particular product, such as side effects or expiration date of a product, can be held liable for noncompliance of the Consumer Protection Act. This act covers a wide variety of issues regarding transactions between businesses and individuals.

Sometimes it is difficult to determine the level of responsibility between the manufacturer, distributor, or retailer when it comes to product liability. In some cases, the manufacturer can be held liable for design or manufacturing defects of the product, but keep in mind that retailers are the consumers' direct contact when it comes to product liability grievances. The consumer bought the product from your online retail store, and in the event of a grievance, you and/or your business are in the direct line of sight. There is the possibility that a buyer will blame you for selling the product to them, even if you sold it in good faith.

The best way to protect your business from product liability entanglements is to deal with a reputable vendor or distributor. Make sure that the online product description is accurate, and make sure that the product you ship to the customer matches the product you sell on your website. Ensure that warranties are enclosed with the product. Your website should also state the product warranty in close proximity to the product, or it should provide a link that will give warranty details. Disclosures of a product (any type of information regarding a product, such as warranties, rebates, etc.) should also be placed in close proximity to the product and product description, or the information should be hyperlinked.

Businesses selling food, cosmetics, and pharmaceuticals are especially vulnerable to product liability issues due to the nature of their products. In this case, obtaining product liability insurance is advisable.

Conducting any type of retail business is a risk, and the key to minimizing the risk involves an analysis of your product's appropriateness for online retail and an assessment of the product's risks to you in terms of your liability should your product potentially cause any injury to the buyer.

Online Pricing Errors

Online pricing errors are very expensive typos or computer glitches. Mistakes in pricing can cost your business a fortune, or they can turn off a potential buyer from purchasing from your site. Unlike a brick-and-mortar store, where pricing errors on merchandise can be caught by a sales representative, online pricing errors are sitting targets waiting for a shopper who will, in good faith, believe that the price is accurate. What will you do if you are selling a $500.00 necklace and it is mistakenly priced at $5.00? What if a customer decides to buy ten of these necklaces? What do you do? If you have wrongly priced an item online, you can protect yourself by having a disclaimer stating that online pricing errors need not be honored by the seller. This is a good idea if you are selling very high-end products and continuing with the transaction can produce a loss. The Equitable Doctrine of Unilateral Mistake allows an online retailer to cancel an order if pricing mistakes can cause a huge loss for the business and if it was a good-faith pricing mistake taken advantage of by unscrupulous online buyers. For instance, if an online buyer purchases 500 computers mistakenly priced at $1.00 and the listed price should have been $1,000.00, then the contract can be deemed void. The catch is that you have to detect this pricing error before the 500 computers are shipped. You can still take some form of legal action against the buyer, but it would be very difficult.

The Smart Customer

My business will occasionally give discount cards to customers offering them $10 off of their entire order. The discount card specifies that they will get a $10 discount on their entire order, which means that if a customer buys five items, $10 will be taken out of the entire order. However, on one batch we experienced a glitch in the system that took $10 off each item that a customer purchased.

We didn't fix the problem because it wasn't really a big deal, and since customers bought high-value items, even a $10 discount per purchased item was almost negligible. From a marketing standpoint, the system glitch seemed to work because we thought that it would garner more sales. The point was that if customers felt that they were getting an "extra deal," they would be encouraged to buy more. We thought that the glitch couldn't do anything to harm our business.

Wrong! As a service to our customers, there is a hidden part of the website that allows them to customize their orders. Customers can choose the size of the pearls they can buy by the inch, and they can customize a necklace or bracelet accordingly. A woman began purchasing pearls by the inch as a single order. She selected a size that cost $8.00 an inch. She placed numerous orders using the discount card. Because her purchase was only $8.00 and the discount card was $10.00, we essentially owed her $2.00. She cleverly took advantage of the system.

We finally had to call her to say that we wouldn't be honoring the order as it stood. From a legal standpoint, we didn't have to fill the order because it wasn't in compliance with the terms of the discount.

The Lesson Learned:

There are always people out there looking for a way to beat the system, and you have to watch out for them. What you might think is a harmless glitch in the system can turn out to be deadly. If you find that your software isn't calculating orders properly, get it fixed—quickly!

Rights of the Business Owner versus Rights of the Customer

Conducting an online business should be a fair exchange between the seller and the buyer. Both have rights in the eyes of the law, and there are just as many unscrupulous buyers as there are unscrupulous businesses. As a business owner, you are vulnerable to customer fraud. Customers can easily claim that a product is defective or that they never received the product. And buyers can fall prey to companies that sell them defective merchandise or merchandise that was never shipped. The rules of ethical business practices have been established to protect the customer. But who will protect you from the customer? Chances are that you just might have more to lose than the malfeasant buyer.

Protecting your business from unethical customers starts with your own business policy. Make sure that the terms, conditions, and shipping policies are clearly stated on your website and/or in your listings. To do this properly, you might want to conduct your own research by examining successful, credible retail websites. Compare and contrast their policies, and draft one that is standard to the retail world, as well as conducive to the capabilities of your online business. If your terms and conditions are clearly stated, you have a better chance of taking legal action against a customer who has broken the terms of agreement between the seller and the buyer. You may take legal action against a customer who has taken advantage of you. However, the financial practicality of hiring a lawyer because of a sales dispute does not always make good business sense, especially if the matter could have been avoided by taking precautions (such as using a secured payment gateway that matches the address of the credit card holder to the shipping destination requested).

As a business owner you have the right to get paid by the customer who purchases your product, and any returns should be made in compliance with the terms and conditions stated on your website.

Illegal Products

If you want to have a legitimate business, then sell legal products. Do not sell unauthorized copies (bootlegs) of DVDs, CDs, and/or books or print material. Do not sell any illegal drugs or paraphernalia, or objectionable adult-themed products.

The Digital Millennium Copyright Act, a US copyright law signed by President Bill Clinton on October 28, 1998, is a bill that focuses on antipiracy laws. Piracy was becoming, and still is, prevalent on the Internet.

Selling legitimate products will keep you in business for the long-term. Selling illegal products will keep you in the clink, or at the very least in the poorhouse once you're caught and forced to pay a hefty fine.

Ethics

Good online ethics are good business ethics. There has been much debate about what can be said and done in the online world, but as far as online retail goes, a good customer service policy that the merchant lives up to is the key to good business and good sales. The World Wide Web is comprised of various cultures, and while the values of different cultures might vary, we should recognize that the growth of the Internet and the World Wide Web constitutes a remarkable potential for people to make money the right way. As an online retailer, keep your promise to the customer, ship the actual orders and avoid pricing errors, provide good-quality products, and deliver them free of damage. Do not sell products that can harm or endanger the consumer.

E-mail spamming is a nuisance, but it is also considered unethical in many circles and is often illegal. Spammed e-mail addresses are usually obtained from databases, bulletin board postings, or spammers simply guess them. Spam e-mails are like junk mail—they are more of a nuisance than anything else—but the obtaining of the domain names is what remains suspect. Unsolicited e-mails from unknown senders can also carry computer viruses. Don't become a plague to people who might otherwise become potential customers. This advice holds true for advertising through your Facebook or your Twitter pages. It is okay to market your products, but do not spam your potential customers! If you "post" or "Tweet" all day long about your items, you will lose "fans" and "followers" and likely find yourself out of business. Find a healthy balance of timing and marketing of your products along with posting useful information to your customers.

Good behavior requires good ethics. A good business owner practices good ethics, and in return, the credibility of the business grows. Do not use unethical means to gain traffic to your website; in the long run, they just do not work.

Most of all, remember that what you put on your web page is a representation of you as the business owner. Conduct your business with the dignity and professionalism befitting of a legitimate, successful entrepreneur, and you will reap the benefits of success.

06

The Internet and E-Commerce

The Internet has revolutionized the way we live our lives. Everything in the world is practically a point and a click away. Today over one billion people use the Internet worldwide. When was the last time you actually wrote a letter to a friend and mailed it without using your computer? In the United States, 77.3 percent of the population is online (ITU, 2010). If we want information about umbrellas, it is just a matter of typing in the keyword and a gazillion web pages will show up. We can chat with someone who sells umbrellas in another state or in another country. Moreover, getting information is much easier today because of the Internet. The Internet has made everything so convenient that many of us would probably be paralyzed without it.

Most of all, the Internet has changed the way consumers shop. Face it, online shopping is here to stay, and we should all be thankful for that. There is a lot of money to be made in online retail, especially home-based online businesses, because the overhead is low. The competition is tough, online sites are fighting for top rankings in searches, and search engine optimization (SEO) has become the new catchphrase of online retail. That's why finding out how the Internet works is a key component to the preliminary research you must do before launching your business.

The Internet and the World Wide Web

The Internet is a complex network that links other computer networks. Think of the Internet as a very intricate spiderweb and every cross section of that web is a computer. The origins of the Internet began in 1969 when the US military created the ARPAnet (Advanced Research Project Agency Network), a system that allowed the military to reroute messages in the event that hostile forces attacked portions of their network. This connection of networks is the basis for the Internet today, and although the Internet is no longer exclusive to the military, it has become an important means by which individuals, institutions, and companies communicate. Although the Internet is still a source of information, it has become a home for commerce. In 1996 the Internet became available to the public. There would be no e-mail, chat, websites, or e-commerce without the Internet, and I wouldn't have written this book. We can make various online transactions, and this has made life a lot easier. In fact, we do not even have to leave the house because we can get our groceries delivered, we can order pizza, we can even find a date online. The Internet has made living in front of a computer a way of life.

In the past, if we wanted to buy something, we either had to go to a store or order from a catalog. Today, all we need is a personal computer and Internet connection, and our next purchase is just a click away. Someone sitting in front of a computer that has Internet access can purchase just about anything his or her credit card limit will allow.

The World Wide Web (WWW) is not to be confused with the Internet. The WWW is an interconnected set of websites linked together by a hyperlink, a sort of reference that lets the computer know where a web document is located. The Internet basically connects your computer to the billions of websites that comprise the WWW. The WWW began with an idea by Tim Berners-Lee, who built the first web browser, a software application allowing the user to show and access web pages. As with all great ideas, Berners-Lee's idea came out of necessity. While he was working for CERN, he wanted to be able to access CERN's huge directory easily. The problem was that everything was stored in different databases, and that made information retrieval difficult. So he designed the first web browser (a web browser is located in the upper section of a website). This idea eventually grew into what the WWW is

Did You Know . . . ?

The Internet with a capital "I" refers to the specific name of the Internet as a whole.

The internet with a small "i" refers to the network of interconnected local area networks.

today. The WWW became available to the public in 1991, but it gained worldwide popularity in 1993 when CERN announced that the public would be able to access the WWW for free.

Search Engines

Search engines are a key element in conducting online research, especially for business owners. In this modern age of Google, Yahoo, MSN, and various other websites, search engines can "do the walking for you" when it comes to finding information. A search engine is basically a program that helps the Internet user find information on the WWW. Alan Emtage, who was a student at McGill University in Montreal in 1990, created the first Internet search engine, which he named "Archie." Emtage created the Archie search engine to index directory listings in order to easily find information on file names. Mark McCahill, a student at the University of Minnesota during the mid-to late 1970s, received his degree in chemistry in 1979. McCahill later joined the university's computer center as a programmer in Apple II and CDC Cyber programming. In 1991 he led the development team that created a search engine—which McCahill named "Gopher"—that indexed text files. This was the beginning of the first websites because indexing text files is similar to indexing websites. Websites in the WWW are accessed by the web crawler of the search engine. The website content is then evaluated by the web crawler for indexing (you might think of this as categorizing the websites). When a user types in a keyword, the search engine looks for the relevant words within the indexed files, usually through the title of the web page or through the first section or paragraph of a website. The following is a list of popular search engines:

- Google
- Yahoo
- MSN
- Bing

Search Engine Optimization (SEO)

The method of creating a website that ranks high in a search engine result.

How can knowledge about search engines help your online business? Well, consumers who buy online tend to search the keyword of the product they want to buy. After the query, pages are ranked in the search results, and online business owners should understand that optimizing website content helps the website rank higher in the search results. So, if you want to search domain names, consider the first ten websites ranked. You might notice that some of them are commercial websites that offer services for domain name registration. Sometimes websites pay the search engine company so that their site ranks higher, or some sites pay an advertising fee. "Sponsored Links" are commercial sites that have paid for advertisement. They usually show up on the right-hand side of the web page. In any case, evaluate the sites that show up in the first thirty rankings and study how they are written. Are the service descriptions clear? Does the site give too much information to the point of confusion, or is it just enough to tickle the curiosity of the reader? These are things you should consider when writing your website. Remember, although search engines cannot help your online business, knowing how a search engine works will help you in designing your website.

The following is a list of shopping portals that deal strictly with online retail. Although they are not as popular as Google or Yahoo, these sites can prove useful in your online research.

- Amazon.com
- eBay.com
- Shopping.com
- NexTag.com
- Buy.com
- Barnes&Noble.com
- Etsy.com
- Addoway.com

Expert Tip

Don't focus on making money, focus on being successful. If you are successful, money will follow.

Web Browsers

When you are surfing the Net, you are using a web browser. A web browser helps you travel the WWW in search of whatever it is you are looking for. It helps you retrieve information published in web pages, and it also helps you transmit information. A web browser, the most common type of HTTP user agent, allows users to access different websites on the WWW. The following are the most popular web browsers available to the public:

- Microsoft Internet Explorer
- Mozilla Firefox
- Google Chrome
- Apple Safari
- Opera

E-Commerce

E-commerce is the term for any type of transaction that occurs via the WWW. Transactions ranging from filing income taxes, making hotel reservations, and buying and trading stock to purchasing items are part of the e-commerce world. The secret of e-commerce is in building customer trust. Successful e-commerce sites let the customer know that the transaction is secure, and credit card information sent through is encrypted. Most e-commerce businesses understand that website design and keeping up with the latest technology available to online businesses are just a few ways to stay ahead of the competition. However, despite the success of e-commerce in the past ten years, start-up businesses still experience e-commerce problems. These problems are similar to the issues of commerce in the brick-and-mortar world. Lack of planning, underestimating the competition, and failing to understand the target market are just a few factors that prevent the success of an e-commerce venture. Nevertheless, the number of e-commerce sites is growing, and the opportunities to be had in this business genre are open to those who understand that a successful online business is just like a brick-and-mortar store, except that you don't have to tidy up the merchandise after the last customer leaves, and customer service means making the online shopping experience easy, convenient, and safe. When e-commerce took off in 1994, strategists predicted that e-commerce would change the face of business transactions. Despite the dot-com debacle in 2000, online companies have learned their lesson in realizing that business and financial planning are just as important in the online world as they are in the brick-and-mortar world.

E-Retail

Electronic retail, also known as e-retail or e-tail, is a type of e-commerce, specifically about selling one product to a consumer via the WWW. With the influx of online retail businesses, it is difficult to gain an audience unless the entrepreneur determines a product niche and a savvy way to sell the product. Online retailers have a gamut of

How I Discovered Online Retail

When I first decided to sell pearls in 1996, the Internet didn't even cross my mind. I was actually looking for locations in my hometown of Washington. The area where I lived was pretty small, and there wasn't really a large market for pearls. Moreover, I realized that even if I did open a jewelry store for pearls, the rent alone would have eaten away at my profit, and being located in a particular area actually limited my customer base.

I had Internet connection at the time, and there were some online retail stores, so I decided to try it out. What I found with the Internet and what I am still finding today is that my customer base is constantly expanding. I literally sell to the world. As more and more people become comfortable shopping online and buying higher-priced items (I have actually purchased two cars online), online retail will continue to grow.

The Lesson Learned:
The Internet gave me access to the world, and it gave the world access to me.

products to choose from, but merchandise with a high value-to-weight ratio, such as books, CDs, DVDs, jewelry, computer software and accessories, and clothing and accessories are good products to sell online because shipping costs are minimal. One of the detriments of online shopping is the cost of shipping to the buyer, and although buyers know that shipping is part of the deal, some customers are aghast by some shipping-and-handling costs. In the past ten years, there has been an influx of brick-and-mortar stores that have established online retail sites. Stores such as the Gap, Nordstrom's, Target, and Barnes & Noble were primarily brick-and-mortars that have established another genre in their business online. Brick-and-mortars understand that there is a lot of money to be made in online shopping, and online retail doesn't require the labor capital that offline retail stores can demand. Moreover, more and more people are shopping online, and successful brick-and-mortars know that business competition is not only about product and price, but also about capturing a new customer base—a customer base that lets the computer do the walking. Nevertheless, despite the growing popularity of online retail, there are still customer concerns about purchasing online:

- Information security
- Trust
- Shipping costs
- Lack of person-to-person interaction

10 Reasons Why Online Businesses Succeed

1. Customer-friendly website
2. Viable product niche
3. Competitive customer service policy
4. Quality merchandise
5. Timely shipping
6. Ability to understand target audience
7. Attractive website
8. Flexible to changing markets and customer demands
9. Use of cutting-edge technology
10. Competitive pricing

10 Reasons Why Online Businesses Fail

1. Unattractive website
2. Failure to understand target audience
3. Failure to understand the competition
4. Failure to adapt to market change
5. Poor business and financial planning
6. Noncompetitive pricing
7. Failure to establish customer trust
8. Poor customer service policy
9. Failure to establish a product niche
10. Poor-quality merchandise

These concerns are reasonable, and start-up online businesses must deal with these issues. Online retailers deal with these issues by creating websites that have aesthetic and emotional appeal.

Attractive websites that are easy to navigate are able to keep potential buyers on the site for longer periods of time. Imagine the retail website as a brick-and-mortar store. If you enter a store with a poor layout and badly displayed products, would you be compelled to buy anything from such a place? Chances are the answer to that question would be "no." It's the same in the online world. A poorly designed website without visual appeal will not attract customers. Successful online retailers know that customers who return to the site will eventually buy from the site. Moreover, if a customer can easily click in and out of your website's various pages, and if the customer stays on your website long enough, then that customer just might click themselves into purchasing from your site.

However, a good-looking site is not enough. Consumers want to feel secure when making their online purchases—they want assurance that their privacy and financial information are protected. Today, online consumers know about the various security measures available on reputable retail sites. Security measures such as Verisign assure the online consumer that any information they release during the process of their online transaction is safe and secure. This security measure is usually carried out through an encryption process. This is a protocol in most "secure" transactions. Online retailers will usually display various online safety measures they abide by. For instance, when you go to my site PearlParadise.com, you will find four online safety measures displayed on the front page of the site. This reassures buyers that it's safe to purchase from the site. It gives them the needed security and trust they need to feel before they make a purchase on the site.

Shipping is another issue in online retail. Many consumers do not like to pay for shipping, nor do they like to wait for products to arrive. One way to deal with these issues is to emphasize the savings that buyers can enjoy in purchasing from the site. If customers believe that your site is the only source for a particular product at a price that is attractive to them, then chances are customers will not mind having to pay for shipping.

Perhaps the biggest challenge that online entrepreneurs face is the lack of person-to-person interaction. What successful online entrepreneurs do is let the website do the talking for them. The most important aspect of online retail is the website. Your website is the face of your business, and it must be able to communicate to the buyer that shopping at your website means that they are getting a quality product at a good deal. It should also give your customers a sense of safety. Websites that are secure for credit card purchases are important, and your website should communicate your commitment to guarding customers' financial information and privacy. Successful online retail businesses take the business seriously.

Researching the WWW

Now that you have a basic knowledge of the difference between the Internet and the WWW, let us talk about how you can use the WWW to find out what you need to know. Remember that the WWW is rich with information and you can find out just about anything by typing in a keyword. However, be discriminating when you conduct your research. When researching a particular subject, make sure that you conduct what I call "redundant research." Do not take the word of one website as fact. Check out three to five different websites about the subject, then compare the information. Recurring information from different sites gives you an idea of the trend of the subject you are querying. When researching the product you would like to sell online, check out the websites listed on one of the shopping search engines I mentioned earlier in the chapter. In researching your product, you will need to inquire about the following:

- General information about the product
- Price range of the product
- Who is selling the product

When researching possible sources for domain name registration, website designers, and credit card account providers (which we'll address in chapter 10), you will be looking for sales organizations offering services. Make sure that you talk to account representatives after you have studied their websites. Nothing really replaces the human element, especially when it comes to price and service comparison. Here are some general categories of search engines:

- General search engines
- Meta search engines
- Pay-per-click search engines
- Google-based search engines
- Yahoo-based search engines
- Shopping search engines
- News search engines

Impact of the Internet

We can vicariously experience the whole world by sitting in front of our computer monitor. Whoever thought that we would spend billions on products sold online? And whoever thought that the Internet would spawn the information revolution? The Internet's impact on education will revolutionize the way we learn. Will teachers ever be phased out of the classroom in lieu of lessons and lectures accessible on the Internet? I hope not, because as fascinating and influential as the Internet has been, human interaction is still a vital part of our existence. I, for one, am an avid fan of the Internet, and its impact on my life has been tremendous. Nevertheless, behind all that network connection, amidst the wires and cable, the human element is the force behind the technology.

What Is "Going Live?"

"Going live" is the process of having a fully functioning website that the public can access.

07

What You Need to Know about Creating Your Website

Website design and content are everything to an online retailer. Your website is your main tool of communication in the online retail world. The look and content of your website is how you will attract customers, and it is how you can get them to buy from you. Remember that online shoppers have a short attention span, and a website that looks confusing will just turn customers off. They can just as easily click out of your site as they can click in. A good retail website should look good, it should communicate to the target customers the message you want to convey, it should have a unique style that stands out from other websites, and it should be easy to navigate. A customer-friendly website is the glue that will keep the potential buyer stuck to your site. What you want to do is generate interest, and interested customers will keep looking through your site until you finally hook them with a sale. You do not have to be an expert in web design to be an online retailer, but you need to have a basic knowledge of website design and content even if you plan to hire a web designer to create your website. Your website will ultimately be your vision of how you want to represent your online business to your potential customers.

Getting Started

When I started my business, I knew how to turn on the computer—that was it! I had no technical background, but I had friends who were technically savvy. I remember thinking that I would never want a job that required me to stare at a computer screen all day (how ironic). It was a task for me just to place auctions on Amazon.com, and building a website to sell my product seemed completely out of my reach. I was wrong.

I did some research before I began to build my website. I found that there are tools such as program templates available to someone like me that would allow me to build a site from scratch without learning complex computer code. I quickly realized that having the knowledge or working with someone with programming knowledge would be important as my business started to grow. I found that there were websites that offered template services. Templates are ready-made design options. I simply needed to add product information, choose colors and fonts, and follow the instructions laid out for me. So, I did. I learned how to upload product photos and descriptions, and in the end I learned quite a bit about website design. I had a fully functioning website within a week. I was able to accept credit card orders, and I was proud that I was actually able to do something so technical. Having a fully functioning store that I built for a couple of hundred dollars within a week could not have been done in the "real world." There are still various expenses associated with having a website, but it will always be much cheaper than owning a brick-and-mortar store.

Using a template has its advantages and disadvantages. Templates are simple to use, and if you are on a shoestring budget, they are a good option. If you decide to use templates, try to learn how to use software such as Dreamweaver, which will give you more design flexibility. If you do use templates, make sure that the program you choose gives you some options for designing some of the pages yourself. Using templates allows you to alter pages at your own discretion. If you go with a hosting company that offers "ready-to-go sites," you have less control because your only access to your website is through a separate interface that limits your control over the coding. Nevertheless, whether you are designing your site from scratch or you are using templates, it is important to make sure your site is user-friendly and easy to navigate.

Creation is a process of discovery, and although you most likely have often cruised the web, now is the time to really "look at what you're seeing" in terms of

Template Pros and Cons

Pros
- Easy to use
- Cheap
- You can do it yourself

Cons
- Limits your design
- Hard to optimize

how online retail websites look and what they say about the product. So, before you begin creating your website, ask yourself the following questions:

- Who is my target market?
- What is my budget for my website?
- Will I be able to write the content (such as product description and company information) myself, or will I need to hire someone to write it for me?
- Do I know enough about web design to create the website myself?
- Who is my competition?
- What are the pertinent keywords that potential customers would use to look for the type of product that I am selling?
- How many graphics do I need or want in the website?

Think about the subjective and objective goals you have for your website. The subjective goal is your own aesthetic sense of what you want your website to look like.

- What type of colors do you like?
- How many graphics do you want to incorporate in your website?
- How much product description do you want next to the picture of the product you are selling?
- What type of font do you want to use, and what size font should it be?
- How do I want customers to navigate the site?

The objective goal is to design a site that will appeal to your customers. Objective goals deal with the following:

- Is the website easy to navigate?
- Does the website have enough product information?
- Does the website look professional?
- Can the website attract the attention of customers through graphics and product description?
- Does the website have too many graphic elements or not enough?
- Do you have enough security measures on the website to gain the customer's trust?
- Does the overall look of your website appeal to your target customer?

What looks good to you might not look good to others, and balancing your subjective and objective goals is a good way to start the pre–website design process.

Research the Competition

Before you embark on a website design strategy, check out your competition and be sure to keep in mind the questions you have asked yourself and the goals you have set. Begin by making a list of possible keywords or phrases that a potential customer would use when looking for your type of product. Then type in each keyword to the more popular search engines such as Google, Yahoo, and MSN—check out the results. A high ranking on a search engine list does not necessarily mean that the particular online retail website is making money, but it lets you know the type of websites that customers will see first in the search results. Look at the first ten to twenty results on a given keyword/phrase for each search engine. Are there any sites that consistently rank in the top twenty? Look at the features on the website and notice where the keyword first appears. For instance, the keyword search for PearlParadise.com is "pearl jewelry." When you search this keyword on Google and Yahoo, PearlParadise.com usually receives a second or third ranking. On the website, you will notice that the word "pearl jewelry" appears as the top heading on the menu items. Browse through the various online retail sites and compare and contrast their sites. Then ask yourself the following questions:

- Which sites visually appeal to me the most?
- Which sites are easy to navigate (customer-friendly)?
- What are the shipping and return policies of the sites?
- Which sites are selling the exact product I plan to sell?
- What are their price points?
- What is their customer service policy?

It is not a good idea to copy or "mirror" these sites, but this train of thought guides you to understand how other people are doing it, and you may want to take a similar or different approach. Take notes on what you see, then think about the overall composition of the type of website you want to create. There are a variety of website programs, templates, and tutorials that can help you get started. Even if you opt to hire a web designer, you can save time and money if you have a basic idea of what you want your site to look like. Your website will need pictures of the various products you want to sell, along with the description and price of the product. How you want to design the placement of your products will be up to you. In researching other online retail sites, remember how you felt while navigating the sites. Did you find what you were looking for easily? Did you get frustrated? What did you think about the look of the site? Chances are good that this research will give you an idea of the type of website design that works for you, as well as what might work for your customer.

Web Design Programs

Dreamweaver

A template program that allows you to create web pages—good for do-it-yourselfers.

- Allows user to create websites and web pages.
- Allows user to use basic JavaScript without prior coding knowledge.
- Allows user to replace lines of text or code.
- Available for both MAC and Windows.
- 80 percent of HTML text uses Dreamweaver.
- Popular feature "Extensions" allows for flexibility in site structure.
- Allows users to connect to databases for use of scripting programs.

This program has been criticized by some web developers because the program tends to create large HTML pages that have a tendency to load improperly, and some of the codes do not comply with W3C (World Wide Web Consortium) standards. Dreamweaver has attempted to solve this issue in recent years. Despite some of its problems, Dreamweaver's popularity makes this program a good bet for designing web pages.

> **World Wide Web Consortium (W3C)**
>
> An organization founded by Tim Berners-Lee for the purpose of developing a conformance protocol to improve the compatibility of HTML programs developed by different vendors.

Adobe Photoshop

Allows the user to create digital photographs and images—used by both amateurs and professionals.

- Two versions of Adobe Photoshop available for MAC and Windows.
- Allows user to edit images and pictures.

Photoshop controversy delves into the user being able to alter images, but this program is generally used by nearly all online retailers. Photoshop is usually used to remove backgrounds, sharpen images, and design graphics. Nevertheless, some unethical retailers will Photoshop an image to make it look better than the actual product itself, which is a form of false representation. For instance, if you took a picture of your product and that picture needed to be altered so that the product would show up more clearly, Photoshop provides a way to clean up the image and make it clearer. "Photoshopping" an image to fool consumers about the quality, size, or actual look of the product is false representation.

Flash

Allows users to create graphics and animation.

- Most commonly used for advertisements.
- Used by artists to showcase their work.

Most online retailers who wish to be read by the search engines do not generally use Flash unless the home page is integrated with HTML text. This program can also create problems for customers using older computers because their computers might not be able to download the latest version of Flash Player to view the Flash site. Flash creates a great-looking web page or site, but its practical function to the online retailer is minimal. Whether or not you use Flash in your website depends on the nature of your product. In my case, selling pearl jewelry online doesn't require the use of Flash, but if you're into selling DVD games, you might want to create an animated site to echo the theme of your products.

Website Content

Conflict between the design and content of a site often occurs during the creation process of a website. There is often friction when it comes to designing a really cool-looking website versus an easily navigable website that is consumer-friendly. Graphics might be aesthetically appealing, but content is what will keep the customers in your site. Part of your sales hook is giving the customer as much information possible about the product you are selling. This is done to garner customer trust and interest. A good web designer will design a website that is easy to navigate and is customer- and search engine–friendly. A good designer will also consider the content that must be put into your website. Websites done strictly in Flash might have the graphic pizzazz, but search engines do not tend to index Flash sites. Although there are ways to design a Flash site that is search engine–friendly, most serious online retailers will stay away from sites done exclusively in Flash.

Establishing website credibility is done through graphics, product information, and showing the customer that it is safe to shop on the site. A synergy between high-quality graphics and good content satisfies the need for both the visual and intellectual appeal of your website. Remember that you are doing this to make money. As an online retailer, you want to showcase your product. You do not need anything flashy—flashy websites are usually a means for artists to showcase their work. What you need to get the most customer traffic is a website that receives top ranking on a keyword search.

Visual Presentation

That's not to say that the look and feel of your website isn't just as important as the content. In fact, the colors, layout, and font are the factors that will give your website the visual appeal that will compel the potential customer to continue looking. Designing your retail website warrants the use of photos. Using stock photos or photos that you have taken yourself is up to you, but keep the background of the picture consistent. Don't have a white background in one picture and a gray background in another. This looks unprofessional and it tends to distract buyers' attention from your product. If you look at my website PearlParadise.com, the background color in my product display is consistent. Consistent background allows the customer to view the product without being disrupted by inconsistent background that can clutter the look of a page.

Do you prefer a traditional website structure or something unique? Be careful that your innovation does not distract from the actual focus of the site—your product. Also consider the contrast of colors in your website. This is up to your own aesthetic preference, but it is a good idea to get a variety of opinions. Should you have a busy-looking website that lists everything on the same page, or will you break it up in several web pages? You will develop a sense of what you like and what looks good to you, but you are not your customer—keep in mind what looks good to others as well.

Search Engine Optimization (SEO)

Search engine optimization, or website optimization, is the process of improving the page ranking of your website in a search engine result. A page ranking shows the order of sites that are listed in a keyword search from top (highest) to bottom (lowest). This is a key component to ultimate success in online retailing. Your website is the home of your site, and web pages are the various pages that are contained in your website. A home page is similar to a book's table of contents. Optimize not only your home page, but the various web pages in your site as well. You want to increase a customer's point of entry into your site, and optimized pages increase your ranking. The higher your website ranks in search engines, the more visitors your website will receive because users of the WWW rarely go beyond the first thirty results in a keyword query. Most users usually search through Google, Yahoo, or Bing. There are other search engines out there, but the page results are mostly copies of the major search engines that I have mentioned above. Since Google, Yahoo, and Bing are the most popular, this section will discuss their page-ranking guidelines, along with search engine optimization basics that every online retailer should know.

How Search Engines Work

There are two types of search engines you can use when conducting a search: directory-based search engines and spider-based search engines. Each ranks website pages differently, requiring different optimization strategies.

- **Directory-based search engines** function much like a telephone directory. They conduct their searches using title, category, description, and keyword form fields that describe a website. When you submit information to Yahoo

Directory or DMOZ, your keyword form fields (a list of keywords that are thematically connected) may be edited by the directory editor. Changes in your web pages don't affect your search ranking with this type of search engine.

- **Spider-based search engines** rank websites by using "spiders" or "web crawlers" to search the website for visible text (what the customers will see—titles and headings) and invisible text (codes in the title page and link structures—meta tags). This type of search engine is not human-powered, and changes in web pages can affect search ranking. Spider-based search engines such as Google also determine page ranking according to the usability, content, and size of the site.

- **Hybrid search engines** employ more than one form of "meta data" to display results in a keyword search. A directory-based and spider-based search engine is considered a form of meta data. Hybrid search engines can use combinations of meta data. They are the latest in search engine modification.

Web page optimization should consider search engines' methods and function to properly optimize a site.

Some Good Luck!

In 2002 I told a friend that my organic search ranking was not as high as I expected it to be. Luckily, he introduced me to a site called localsubmit.com. I talked to the representative, and I hired him for a six-month contract as a search engine optimizer. The whole thing cost me $1,500 at the time. He optimized my site, and within two months I was on top of the search engine ranking. Although this was done four years ago, PearlParadise.com continues to rank in the top three in Google and Yahoo organic search results. The reason for this is that he didn't over optimize my website. He followed what was called the "white-hat" (ethical and within the guidelines of search engines) way of optimization. Search engines tend to rank you lower or boot your out of their listings altogether if they think that you've tried to cheat their system. He didn't over optimize my site, but he did do a quality job. Today, it will take about six months to build your site rankings (because search engines now rank your site in terms of user and link popularity), but the optimization method that localsubmit.com used on my site four years ago still pertains today. When you are looking to optimize your site, make sure that you approach ethical search engine optimizers.

Basic Guidelines for Search Engine Optimization

Search engines are constantly improving their search ability, and while optimizing your website improves your search rankings, most search engine companies do not like over optimized websites because they can be a form of search engine spamming. If you decide to hire a web designer/developer to create your website, choose one that offers both web design and web hosting, such as www.anysite.be or www.localsubmit.com. These two websites offer free consultation and their fees are reasonable.

Be wary of search engine optimizers who promise you the world when it comes to optimizing your website. Optimizers who try to trick the system by using unethical means of optimization will only do damage to your website in the long run; a search engine will detect their various unethical methods and will give your page a lower ranking or remove it altogether.

For example, some optimizers will fill your website content with hidden or invisible text. This is done by typing keywords that are the same color as the background. These keywords cannot be seen by the human eye, but search engines are able to detect them. The purpose of this is to add more keywords that will show up in more searches. The problem is that search engines can lower your ranking. Search engine companies want to produce relevant search results for web users, and the advent of content spam (the unethical method of overoptimizing a website) can sometimes make it difficult to produce relevant search results. An over optimized website will only attract the wrong type of traffic. Remember that you want interested browsers on your site.

The following is a list of unethical SEO practices that can lower your ranking. When a search engine detects them, they can take your site out of their directory for further investigation.

- **Doorway Pages,** also known as ghost pages, are invisible text to the human eye, but the text is visible to search engines. Some unethical search engine optimizers will use invisible text to overload a web page so the web page will rank higher in the search.
- **Cloaking** is similar to a doorway page in that it presents different content to the search engine than it does to the user or the browser of the website. This is usually done through invisible codes and keywords.
- **Link Farms** are a group of web pages that connect with each other. Many SEOs will sell link farms to e-retailers with the hope that hyperlinks will get them placed higher in a search engine ranking.

Just Say No to Link Farms!

In 1999 search engine optimizers developed the linking of various web pages to take advantage of the Inktomi search engine's method of indexing through link popularity. Hundreds, if not thousands, of hyperlinked web pages received criticism for engaging in a form of spamming. Unscrupulous webmasters took advantage of link farms by receiving inbound links while they devised a way not to display outbound links. They basically had sites exchange links with them, but they never actually placed reciprocal links on their own sites.

Search engines eventually caught on and began filtering the thematic consistency of links. Websites with inconsistent thematic links were either not indexed or their domain names were taken out of search engine indexes. Today, link farms still exist, but they are frowned upon by ethical search engine optimizers.

Following such practices will actually be detrimental to your search ranking, so steer clear of them.

The best advice I can give you is to create a website that truly represents what you are selling, and optimize the site from that standpoint. You will optimize for keyword, keyword placement, theme, domain name, content, tags, meta tags, and links. The following is a detailed description of how you will optimize the above-mentioned categories:

- **Keywords:** When optimizing your website, keyword placement within the text of your site is imperative. Think about what types of keywords people would use in searching for the type of product you are selling. Keywords that are too general will give you a lower ranking because there is simply too much competition. So, what you need to do is come up with a keyword that is specific enough for the type of product you are selling. In my case, I am in the business of selling pearls. So, a keyword search for "pearls" would be too general because other sites about pearls (not necessarily online retail sites, but sites that contain the word "pearl," such as "Pearl Harbor") would likely show up in the search. But using the keyword "pearl jewelry" is specific enough because people who want to buy pearls would most likely be buying jewelry made of pearls.

Keywords that do not appropriately represent your product can generate the wrong kind of traffic to your website. General keywords tend to produce too many results, and your page ranking will suffer as a result. Using a service such as Wordtracker can help you determine how users are searching for your product. Wordtracker lists the various keywords that potential customers would use and creates a database that determines the frequency of the keyword search. Remember that keyword relevancy affects the quality of traffic on your site. A high-ranking website that attracts the wrong traffic is useless, and it is not efficient, especially if you subscribe to pay-per-click advertising.

Pay-Per-Click Advertising

A method of advertising done online when an ad is placed near the results of an online search. For example, pay-per-click advertisers will bid on a keyword such as "office supplies." When a user types in the search term "office supplies," the pay-per-click advertisement will show up either on the results page as a "Sponsored Ad" or above the search term results. The cost of pay-per-click advertising varies depending on the level of competition over particular keywords as well as on the search engine providing the service.

- **Keyword Placement:** After determining the right keywords to use in your website, placing them in the appropriate areas is crucial to optimizing your website for keyword searches. Place pertinent keywords in the following areas: title page, links, headings, URL, in the first paragraph of text, or in the first twenty-five words of the web page. Notice that on my website, the keyword "pearl jewelry" appears in the first line of the navigation menu section of the home page.
- **Theme:** A theme is what your website is about. If you are selling books, then your website is about books, and the keywords that you use should be consistent with that theme. Theme consistency helps your search engine ranking because search engines look for words or variations of words in ranking your website.
- **Page Name:** Make sure that your domain name contains your main keyword(s) because search engines also index your site through your URL.

Obtaining a high search engine ranking means that a link pointing to your website contains your main keywords.

- **Content:** Good content that incorporates well-chosen keywords increases your page ranking. Search engines index your website according to your keywords, and a content-rich website increases your ranking status. Moreover, users are always using the web for research, and a content-rich website creates credibility and trust in the eyes of potential customers. PearlParadise.com has a section about pearl history and the various types of pearls. The site is intended to educate potential customers about pearls, because information establishes trust in the eyes of the customer, and that increases the chance of making a sale. However, make sure that you do not overwhelm people with too much text. People online want information, but they don't want to be bored with too much information, so keep the content short, lively, and informative.
- **Tags:** Tags are keywords or titles on your web page. In written text, a tag should be the first sentence that includes the pertinent keywords that your website is categorized under.
- **Meta Tags:** HTML elements known as meta tags are codes that indicate the content structure of a web page. There are different codes indicating a title, description, keyword, and the beginning and end of a sentence. In recent years, overuse of meta tagging has been frowned upon as an unethical way of optimizing a web page; this is due to "black-hat" search engine optimizers who over optimize a page with invisible text to improve a website's ranking. Not all search engines employ meta tags in their searches, but they can still be an effective way of indexing your website. Remember, meta tags are necessary, but too many meta tags is a form of bad search engine optimization.
- **Page URLs for Different Category Pages:** Create a different URL for each web page in your website.

Linking

Websites such as Google determine rank by popularity. PearlParadise.com ranks number one because of our links. One way to increase your website's popularity is through linking. Linking is the method of providing thematically consistent links within your web page. This method is good for two reasons—it can help increase the popularity of your website, and it increases the amount of traffic you receive.

- **Internal Links** are links within your website. They consist of the various interconnected web pages within your website.
- **Inbound Links** are links to your website from other sites. Inbound links should be thematically consistent with your website, and the header should contain your chosen keyword(s).
- **Outbound Links** are links that go out of your website into another website with a similar theme.
- **Reciprocal Links,** or mutual links, are links made in agreement with other sites.
- **Natural Links** are combinations of one-way links, triangular links, reciprocal link exchanges, and directory links. Natural linking is currently the most effective way of improving your search engine ranking.

> **One-Way Links:** There are two types of one-way links:
> 1. A link to a website (that is an authority in your market) without a reciprocal link to your website.
> 2. You request or pay a website owner to place a one-way link to your website without a reciprocal link to their website.
>
> **Link Exchanges:** Reciprocal links.
> **Triangular Links:** Your website links to website A, and website B (same owner as website A) places a link to your website.
> **Directory Links:** Links that go to a directory.

The synergistic effect of the above links establishes the popularity of your website in the eyes of search engines, and it also gives your website an added service to your customers. It might seem that the links out of your website will take potential customers away, but the effect is that the customer will trust the credibility of your website, and that customer will most likely come back. Linking is common in the Internet world, and it is especially common in optimized websites. Moreover, links can open in another window so that your website stays on the screen. PearlParadise .com has a link feature comprised of mutual links from other sites.

Site Map

Having a site map (a list of navigational menu items that link to particular pages within your site) increases your ranking because it helps the search engines index your website and it helps customers navigate your site.

Optimizing your website is not difficult, but it requires planning. Remember that keywords/phrases, theme, and content allow search engines to read what is in your site, which can increase your ranking status. Knowing the search methods of popular search engines will help you determine which strategy to take in designing your website. Do not try to cheat the search engine by filling your website with invisible text full of keywords—search engines can detect this and they will only give your website a lower ranking.

Elements of Bad Web Design

You do not have to be a webmaster to detect a badly designed website. Just surf the Net and you will encounter a myriad of them. Small sites, sites with too many typos, and sites that look too confusing are badly designed sites. The following is a list of features of poorly designed websites.

- **Unhighlighted Links:** The website should indicate which links have been visited so that a buyer does not unknowingly visit the same page twice. Users are usually irritated by websites that do not highlight previously visited links.
- **Small Font Size:** Small font size can make the text of a website hard to read. Users who find it difficult to read links, product description, and product price will quickly click out of the site.
- **Dense Text:** Online text should be concise, with short sentences and short paragraphs. A 250–300 word count is sufficient. Product description should stick to the pertinent information about the product. Avoid flowery sentences, big words, and links to or selections from articles that do not pertain to your product.
- **Page Titles without Meta Tags:** Search engines such as Yahoo and Bing use crawlers to identify the title of the page for display in the description section of ranked pages. Page titles without meta tags will not get displayed. But remember that the overuse of meta tags in an effort to cheat search engines will result in a lower ranking for your website.
- **Small Websites:** Online retail websites with limited internal links and poor content are not only boring, they may have a hard time establishing trust with potential buyers. If you have a great-looking web page done in Flash, you might get the customers' attention (for a short while), but chances are

that you will not establish enough trust to get them to buy your product. Trust comes from the amount of information you give customers to let them know that you are serious about your business.

- **Flash:** Flash pages are great, but many strictly e-commerce sites don't employ them as much because it's hard for search engines to read them. Search engines cannot read text embedded in graphics. If you must have a Splash page on your site, make sure that you incorporate HTML content so that search engines have a way of reading your site for content. If you want to have a Splash page as the point of entry to your site, make sure that you have a "skip" button. Bear in mind that some online buyers are actually annoyed by Splash pages.

Splash Page

A web page that usually appears when a website is done using a Flash program. A Splash page will most likely contain graphics, and a point of entry into the front page of the site is indicated on the Splash page. These types of pages are great-looking, but are difficult for search engines to read.

- **JavaScript:** Navigation menus in JavaScript will lower your ranking because search engine robots do not execute JavaScript.
- **Frames:** Avoid frames because it's hard for search engines to index pages embedded in frames. This is, however, not to be confused with the structural frame of your website—that is different. The frames referred to here are the frames within the frames, or "frame sets."

A Word about Frames

Frames are the scrollable sections in a website or web page that can contain links and/or text. Content within frames is not always readable by search engines.

- **Hidden Text:** Hidden text in a website is text that unethical SEOs use to improve the ranking of your site. The downfall of this practice is that, in time, search engines catch on to the hidden text and can ban your site from being ranked. For example, making the text the same color as the background will make the text invisible (or hidden) to browsers and is considered a form of spamming. Some SEOs also use certain codes that will place the text outside the view of browsers, which means that text is visible, but it is out of the browser's viewing area. Search engine companies like Google frown upon hidden text in websites because you are essentially trying to trick the search engine by loading the web page with codes.

- **Redirects:** This happens when the address of your website (URL) is redirected to a nonsearchable page. Redirects most commonly occur when your domain or URL is forwarded to another URL in a frame set.

- **Shopping Carts:** Choose a search engine shopping cart with clean URLs. Shopping carts with dynamic URLs with a "?" and other variables are difficult for websites to index. A search engine–friendly shopping cart provides static URLs with clean codes that allow you to change the title and meta tags of each page. Static URLs allow flexibility and easy site maintenance.

- **Bad Graphics:** Do not use flashy graphics. Be sure to keep pictures of your products consistent in size and background.

Web Hosting

Web hosting services provide you with an online system that allows you to store your website data through the WWW. A web host basically provides you with storage space for your website. The hosting plan you choose determines the amount of bandwidth you have for your website. To put it in simple terms, the more bandwidth you have, the more information you can put into your website, and the more traffic your website can handle. A low bandwidth can crash your site if you have too many visitors. Hosting companies such as www.appliedi.net provide reasonable fees and services. There are various hosting plans available: free hosting, shared hosting, and dedicated hosting.

- **Free Hosting** tends to give you a low bandwidth. It is usually supported by advertisement on your site, which explains why it is free. This plan is not a good idea for online retailers. You want to attract a lot of traffic to your site, and this plan just will not accommodate that.
- **Shared Hosting** allows one website to be on the same server with many other websites. Shared hosting also restricts what you can do on your website, and although it is not accommodating if you want to generate traffic to your site, it is a very good way to start.
- **Dedicated Hosting** is perhaps the most appropriate plan for online retailers. It provides you with enough bandwidth to host thousands of visitors on your site, and you have the freedom to design your site with no worries about bandwidth space. You obtain your own web server that will maintain your site for you. You should use this type of hosting especially when your business grows.

Site Submissions

Now that you have this great website, you need to let the search engines know about it. Submitting your website to the search engines can be done in two ways:

automatically and manually. There are various services that will automatically submit your site (for a fee) to thousands of search engines that use robots or spiders. For search engines such as Yahoo, you can automatically or manually register your domain name, which means that you will fill out forms and submit your website to their search engine. In recent years, some spider-based search engines such as Google have frowned upon sites utilizing auto-submission programs; so, it will benefit you to manually submit and/or register your site to the major search engines. Some people prefer to manually submit a website because it gives them insight into the process of search engine submission; it also gives them more control over the information being submitted. Moreover, it helps the site's rankings because fewer mistakes are made.

An auto-submission program is software that allows you to submit your keywords to search engines. The program usually takes the heading text on your website and submits it to search engines. Manual submission involves having to manually submit your keywords to each search engine one at a time. Most search engine optimizers prefer to submit manually because they find this method to be the most efficient way to optimize sites. Most search engines have guidelines for submission, so manual submissions allow you to comply with those guidelines. While it might not hurt to submit/register your site to the various search engines, the majority of search engines use the searches of either Google or Yahoo, so submitting to these two should actually be sufficient.

Do It Yourself or Hire a Web Designer?

Regardless of whether you decide to design your site yourself or work with a web designer, a delineation of the specifics of your website is necessary—think of it as a draft of your website. Working with a web designer requires that there be a written agreement between you and the designer. Whether you spend a few hundred dollars or a few thousand dollars on your website, a delineation of services rendered by the web designer will clarify the web designer's responsibility, and it will give you an idea of what to expect of the finished product. Moreover, a written contract between you and the web designer is a good idea because it becomes a formal agreement, and if the web designer does not satisfy the terms defined in the agreement, you have a course of action for the breach.

Write down a general description of your site and think about the following issues:

- How many web pages will the site have?
- Who will design the graphics?
- Will you write the text yourself or hire a web copywriter?
- What programs will be used? (Dreamweaver, Photoshop, Flash)
- What will be the style of your website? (contemporary, classic, modern, fun)
- What is the download speed? (This depends on the Internet connection available. Most users have either DSL or cable, but some still have dial-up connection and the design of your website should consider this.)
- Is the web designer capable of optimizing your site?
- What other service (URL submission/registration) does the web designer provide?
- Create a schedule of the work to be done.
- When do you plan to have the site online? Determine a completion schedule for that date.
- When will graphics and content be ready? (This can be determined by the designer or by a third party, but a scheduled delivery date of these components should be written down.)
- When can the basic site structure be reviewed and approved by you?
- How long will revisions take?
- What payment schedule is expected by the designer?
- Ask for discounts—always negotiate!

> "Once you have a listing ready to go live, be sure to double check your listing to make sure it looks like you want it to look. And remember to revisit your listings often to see how they will look to a first time visitor to your site."
> —*Roxanne Mitchell, Owner,* Whatadeal on Bonanza.com, www.bonanza.com/whatadeal

Remember that a detailed agreement is a legal contract when signed by you and the web designer. This prevents misunderstandings, and in the event of a conflict, you will have a document that supports your agreement.

Website Design Dos

- ❏ Keep the design simple and easy to understand for the user.
- ❏ Write clean and short HTML codes.
- ❏ Build interesting pages with a lot of content.
- ❏ Make sure that the title of your website and web page contains your pertinent keywords.
- ❏ Build link popularity with carefully selected sites that have the same theme.
- ❏ If you want to use Flash, combine it with HTML content.

Website Design Don'ts

- ❏ Avoid Splash-only pages.
- ❏ Avoid Flash-only pages.
- ❏ Avoid graphic-only pages.
- ❏ Avoid using frame sets.
- ❏ Avoid using JavaScript.
- ❏ Avoid hidden text (search engines will read this and lower your ranking).
- ❏ Do not try to trick search engines by over optimizing your site.
- ❏ Do not use link farms.
- ❏ Review the content and prices for mistakes and typos.

Notes: _____

_____

_____

_____

Site Maintenance

Maintain your site often (at least once a week). When I started, I updated the site myself. I changed photos, prices, and made content changes. Now, I still write any new articles about pearls my site publishes, but I have someone on my staff update the site for me. In updating your site, make sure that prices are inputted correctly. Incorrect product prices are very costly typos if the original price of the product is $100 and you mark it on your site for $10. Websites that are constantly updated also fare better in search engines.

Some Advice about Spending Your Dollars

Go cheap on things that are not integral parts of your online image. If you are hiring a web designer to create your website, make sure that he or she is the best you can afford. Even if you know the son of a friend who knows how to design a website (I have heard this a thousand times), do not skimp. A well-built site is the foundation for your success. A poorly built website or a poorly optimized website will decrease your chances of success.

It does not matter if you are working out of a kitchen, bedroom, or garage, if your website looks professional, it will immediately give the impression that you are a well-established business. Gaining customer trust is part of your marketing strategy.

Last Words

The Internet is growing so quickly that methods will change as the technology changes. Some people consider website creation to be a daunting task, but I hope that by avoiding the tech jargon and by simplifying the explanation of the design process I have erased some of the mystery behind website design and creation.

How do you get the message to the public that you have a great product to sell? There are many ways to accomplish this task. Many people believe that advertising and marketing are synonymous. This is simply not true. These misguided people will tend to concentrate on advertising and neglect marketing. Neglecting marketing is detrimental to your business because marketing is an important factor in ensuring the growth and maintenance of your business. Advertising is but one part of marketing strategy. Marketing allows you the opportunity to think outside the box. You can use your creativity to design a marketing campaign that suits your product niche and target market.

Advertising

Think of marketing as a big puzzle, and advertising as a piece of that puzzle. Marketing involves the management of your various business activities to disseminate information for the purpose of creating product identity, whereas advertising involves sending a persuasive message to the customer to buy your product. Everything you do for your business will involve some type of marketing strategy, from public relations to product placement.

Marketing

- Methodical execution of various business activities (research, advertising, communication, public relations, promotions, and customer acquisition)

- Addresses a particular demographic (personal)

- Delivers an encouraging message about the product/brand

- Focuses on sales and product identity

Advertising

- Part of marketing

- Impersonal

- Delivers a persuasive message about the product

- Paid announcement that encourages a call to action

- Overt message about the product

- Main focus is sales

- Attempts to close a sale

Advertising, simply put, is a sponsor-paid, public message about a specific product that focuses on a broad or specific demographic. Google's pay-per-click program is a form of advertising. Companies use advertising as a specific "call to action," enticing people to consider the purchase of a specified product or service. There are various advertising options for online businesses, but there are only a few that I have personally found effective.

- **Pay-Per-Click:** This method has worked well for my business, but it can be costly, so it is not something that we do on a constant basis. There is no specified length of time you must subscribe to a pay-per-click ad campaign. You can do it for a day, a month, or a year.

- **Offline Advertising:** This can be an option if the ads are demographically targeted. In the spring, we will occasionally place an ad in bridal magazines to capitalize on the wedding season because weddings and pearls are a classic combination.

Ineffective Advertising Campaigns

- **E-mail Campaigns:** I strongly advise against sending any unsolicited e-mail that might be construed as spam. Most people never read the e-mail or open it, for that matter. Spam filters often catch them and store them in a junk mail folder.

- **Pop-up Ads:** These tend to be annoying, and people click out of them before they can even read what the ad is about. Most computers are equipped with software to block these ads, which you will, in effect, be paying for. Additionally, most consumers consider pop-up ads a form of spam.

- **Banner Ads:** These are usually not effective if you are targeting a specific market, but they can work if your product targets a wide demographic.

Marketing Objectives

A good marketing strategy interconnects advertising, promotions, and public relations as the means of getting the message out to your target public that your company has a great product to sell at competitive prices. Marketing is something that you will consistently be doing throughout the life of your business. Developing a good marketing plan is a key factor in your success as a business owner, and your ability to integrate your marketing philosophy into your business activities makes good business sense.

Marketing has important objectives:

- Create product awareness
- Increase sales
- Create product/brand identity
- Acquire new customers
- Retain customers
- Establish product/brand awareness
- Communicate the brand/product
- Spread product/business information

In e-retail, you have one destination where your customers can go to view your product—your website. The wonderful thing about the online world is that your single destination is just a click away from the entire world. The issue then is, how do you get customers to your website, and how do you get them to buy what you're selling?

Effective online marketing strategy attempts to resolve the above questions. Marketing encompasses nearly all public factors of your business. Previously, I discussed search engine optimization. This is a type of marketing. Managing your website, your product, and yourself are types of marketing activities whose sole purpose is to drive sales, ensure trust, and transport the existing and potential customers to their point of destination (your website). Developing awareness about your product will inform your customers and it will help increase your sales.

Finally, marketing yourself is also important. A big part of my success is the media attention I have received. It might not be an easy task for some people to attract media, but you will be amazed by the extraordinary things that you will do in the process of building your business, and you should share this with the general public through press releases. Anything that you do to draw attention to your product, from demographic research to product brand integrations to press releases, is also part of a marketing campaign. If you've invented a new product, you can generate some good press by informing various trade publications and journals dedicated to your product niche.

Difference between Marketing and Advertising

Advertising involves the placement of an ad and the frequency of that placement. Marketing and advertising must work in conjunction with each other, and while marketing usually becomes a constant presence in your business, advertising might present itself on certain occasions when you want to boost your sales. For example, my company usually advertises on Google's pay-per-click program during the holiday seasons, and we usually advertise in bridal magazines in the spring. There are different forms of marketing and advertising that can help create awareness about your product.

Social networking sites such as Facebook and Twitter are effective ways to create awareness about your business and products. Pay-per-click is a form of online advertising, and getting at the top of an organic search engine result is a form of marketing through your website. The following are a few strategic aspects of marketing:

- **Advertising:**
  Social media
  Pay-per-click campaigns
  Offline advertisements (magazine ads, brochures)

- **Public relations:**
  Getting your story to journalists and editors
  Press releases

- **Website optimization:**
  Keyword optimization
  Link campaigns
  Content-rich pages on the site

- **Product pricing:**
  Competitive prices

- **Product description and photos:**
  Well-written descriptions of your product
  Professional-looking photographs of your products

- **Brand integration and brand awareness:**
  Finding every opportunity to promote your product in the public light
  Making it a recognizable name

- **Community involvement:**
  Supporting a charity on your site
  Donating your product to a high-profile charity

- **Media planning:**
  Selecting the most appropriate media (Internet, print, radio, television) for your product, then designing an advertising campaign

- **E-mail support:**
  Providing timely, friendly responses to customer inquiries
  Utilizing accurate, informational automated e-mail systems (order, payment, and shipping confirmation)

- **Telephone support:**
  Providing friendly, professional telephone support from actual staff, not a call center

An effective marketing campaign employs the various pieces of the puzzle to create an image conducive to increasing sales, building product awareness, and attracting/retaining customers. As you grow your business you will be able to determine which marketing strategies work best for you. It will likely not be necessary to utilize all of the strategies described here. The marketing strategy you use should correlate to the type of business you have.

Market Research

Market research is the process of gathering information in order to learn the trends, behavior, and fluctuations of your product and the consumer. Doing your research makes you a better-informed business owner because you know what is going on in your industry. Research must be done before the business is launched, but you should be constantly market-researching your product once you are in business.

> **Words of Wisdom**
>
> "If we knew what it was we were doing, it would not be called research, would it?"
> —*Albert Einstein*

Learn about Your Market before You Begin Your Business

Before you start your business and begin a marketing campaign, you must first identify the demographics of your target market. In chapter 3 I discussed finding a product that "sells" online. Once you determine your product, then you can determine your target demographics. For instance, I am in the business of selling pearls online. I know that some women like jewelry, especially pearl jewelry, so I know at least the gender of my target market. Gender is one category; next I had to determine the age and socioeconomic status of the women who would buy my pearls. Because I sell pearls at a tremendous discount, I knew that women from all walks of life would be able to afford my product. Nevertheless, I needed to understand how women felt and thought about buying jewelry in general. I had to research the percentage of women who bought jewelry and the circumstances in which they made their purchase. Arming myself with the knowledge of how and why women bought jewelry enabled me to design a website that was appealing to women. If you go to PearlParadise.com, you will notice that the site has muted colors, and the overall look of the site is very soft. I tried to create a site that is conducive to the sensibilities of women. I wanted to create a nice, pleasant-looking site that would "communicate" to the proclivities of women. Now, this doesn't mean that all women react to soft, muted colors, nor does it mean that men do not buy from my site. But my "target" audience is primarily women, so I designed a website that is attractive to them. Our marketing plan for Valentine's Day has the women as an audience, but they will usually tell their husbands and/or boyfriends about the site. Since we offer great savings to the customer, men will often make purchases from our site through the referral of their own wives and girlfriends. You might say that the site attracts women, but there are many instances when men make the purchase.

Knowing who you are selling to will not only help you design a marketing plan, but it will also help you know how you will communicate to your target audience through your website. Market research also helps you position your product so that you can achieve the audience exposure necessary to obtain and build your sales. Creating a product identity is basically done through your website, and knowing who wants your product and who will buy your product is the necessary information that will help you shape the overall tone of your product and business.

Sensibilities of Your Target Audience

In creating an overall marketing plan for your product, you must first identify your target audience. In researching the sensibilities and/or proclivities of your target audience, it is important to first consider the following elements:

- The product

- Price point

- Who wants the product (There may be a difference between the buyer of the product and the market that the product is designed for, especially for children's products.)

- Age range of buyers

- Gender of buyers

Once you have identified the above categories, you can start researching the general identity of your target market. In my case, my product (pearl jewelry) is for women and my site is built to speak to women, which is why my site looks the way it does (as mentioned earlier). I came up with my design by surveying the women I know and researching sites that primarily sell to women. I studied the look of these sites, made comparisons, and concluded that a soft, muted appearance would speak to women. It was not rocket science on my part. I didn't really consult any psychological books or vast surveys to come up with a plan. I knew my product and I knew who my product appealed to—it was that simple.

If your product appeals to both men and women, then you will obviously market the product to both sexes. If your product appeals to women but is bought by men, you will most likely market the product to appeal to women, but the price points must appeal to the men. If your product is for a young audience that does not have spending power (children), you will appeal to the product's intended audience; but again, make the price and information attractive to parents and/or adults buying the item.

Discovering the sensibilities of your target audience in one sense begins with you. As a consumer, what appeals to you? Is it price, convenience, originality? Assess yourself first, then branch out and examine how consumers (men, women, and children, young and old) react to stimulus in your marketing, advertising, and promotions. As I said before, it's not rocket science, but you should read consumer trend magazines and journals and compare their information with your own empirical knowledge.

Continue Your Research throughout the Life of Your Business

Gathering information about sales trends, product development, customer needs, and purchasing patterns is an important part of your business activities. Knowing this will help you understand the "movement" of the various factors that affect your business. There are a variety of programs and services out there that can track your site traffic, customer purchase patterns, and returns. You can also encourage your customers to e-mail their opinion about the product and the website so that you can know what they're thinking. Customer input is valuable, especially in online retail, because person-to-person interaction is practically nonexistent. When you begin your business, sales will be slow and you can basically monitor your customers' behavior through your sales. However, as your business grows and your sales increase, there are programs that you can buy to track your site traffic. These programs can also track what your customers are buying. Tracking your customers' buying behavior lets you know which products are selling and which price points are amenable to your customers. You might even realize that product photos and product descriptions affect your sales. If a product is not moving well, you have the option of removing that particular merchandise from your product line and concentrating on other products that are selling well. You also need to keep abreast of economics and the general trend of your product niche. Basically, you need to know all the variables that will affect your business.

Arthur Charles Nielsen Sr.

Market analyst who founded the idea of market research and established the ACNielsen company, a marketing research firm in 1923. He is best known for establishing the Nielsen Rating, a service that tracks the behavior of television, radio, and newspaper audiences in various markets.

Market research can be conducted in various ways. One way is to read trade journals about your particular product. This will enable you to understand the trends and developments of your demographic market. You can attend local seminars and conventions about your product and absorb the latest trends, news, and developments in the industry. ACNielsen, a marketing research service, is a good source for gathering information about your market. Their marketing research service measures, analyzes, identifies, and diagnoses the pattern and behavior of particular target markets and customers. For more information about the ACNielsen service, log on to www.acnielsen.com. To be a good market researcher, you have to be curious—being inquisitive opens your mind. When you begin your market research, you will gather information on the following:

Product Information

- What is the life span of the product? Is it seasonal, or does it have the potential to be a staple item in the industry?
- Who is selling this product online?
- What are their price points?
- What was the market demand for this product in the past, what is its present market demand, and what will its market demand be in the future?
- Are there any future developments about the product? (Will you be changing or amending your product?)
- When is the product most popular?
- Are there similar products online?

Demographics

- Who is buying the product?
- What is their gender?
- What is their geographical location?
- What is their level of education?
- What is their socioeconomic status?
- Who is the product user?
- Who is the product buyer?
- What are the interests that might connect to the product?
- What are their desires?

Understanding your customer base will help you in developing a product/brand identity, and it will guide you in how you will present the product on your website. Having the answers to the questions from the previous page will help you write the content and determine the type of language that you will use. Also, remember that if there is a difference between the user of your product and the buyers, your website will (essentially) have to communicate with both. For instance, if you are selling toys, your target market will be children and their parents. The intended market for your product will be children, but the buyer will be parents. So, when marketing a product on a website that sells toys, you need to ask yourself, "Who will be viewing my products?" Sometimes there is a difference between buyers and users, especially during the holidays. Also, remember that as your business grows, your product offering will grow as well. When I first started PearlParadise.com I sold necklaces. Now, many years later, we sell necklaces, pendants, bracelets, and earrings, in various styles, shapes, and sizes.

Consumer Behavior

- Why would the consumer buy this product?
- Will consumers buy this product as a necessary item or as a luxury item?
- How does the consumer usually purchase this product? Is it a product that consumers need to see, feel, taste, touch, and hear?
- When do consumers tend to buy this product?
- What product attributes are important to the consumer (price, guarantees, return policy, etc.)?

The behavior and psychology of your customer base will fluctuate depending on the current economic condition. Buying activity also changes during the holiday season and certain occasions such as Valentine's Day and Mother's Day. You will need to alter your marketing in times of economic and market fluctuations. Keeping on top of your customers' buying behavior enables you to alter your marketing strategy.

Competition

- Who is selling this product online and offline?
- Do offline stores selling this product have an online website, and vice versa?
- Which online stores regularly appear in the top ten of an online search engine result?

- What are the price points of these stores?
- What are their customer service, shipping, and payment policies?
- Which websites use pay-per-click ads?

Think of retail (whether online or offline) as a race. Retailers are always striving for the top spot in terms of sales, search rankings, and product/brand awareness. Your challenge as an online retailer is to build your business so that customers connect your business to the product.

Who Is Really Buying, Anyway?

Pearls are typically for women and are bought by women, but men buy pearls as well. They usually buy them as gifts for their wives or girlfriends.

Women who want their husbands or boyfriends to buy them jewelry will tell men about my website. The prices on my website appeal to men, but men also tend to purchase the most expensive item. Why? Because my website has the lowest prices, and when men buy jewelry for women, they want to impress!

On the other hand, you'll notice that my website has a very soft look because I have designed the website to appeal to the female aesthetic.

The website is essentially designed for women, but the prices appeal to men. In this sense, the site speaks to both the buyer and the user of the product.

Acquire New Customers

Catching the attention of a new customer requires some savvy marketing strategies. This is especially challenging because attracting a potential buyer's attention is like going fishing. You need them to bite the bait before you can reel them in. So, how do you get them to bite the bait? First, you need to attract their attention. As I said before, getting them to your website is one way. Once on your website, how will they be enticed by the product? If you don't have the best prices, then you better have something different or unique to offer the customer. Most important is that new customers need to know that your business can be trusted. Make sure that you display any and all security measures that you have on your website. PearlParadise.com has about six different online safety measures and they appear on the front page of the website. I attracted thousands of new customers when I began to receive some media attention a couple of years ago. This gave my business instant credibility, and new customers flooded my site. Attracting new customers can be achieved through the following:

- Search engine optimization
- Competitive prices, customer service, and lenient return policy
- Establishing trust and credibility
- Product/brand integration

Product/Brand Integration Positioning

A marketing technique that positions two different brands or products together for the purpose of capturing the attention of demographics that are not usually exposed to a particular brand or product. The technique is meant to increase exposure and sales. For example, the exposure of Coca-Cola in a movie scene or a television show is product/brand integration.

The film *One, Two, Three* (1961) Stars James Cagney as a Coca Cola executive in West Berlin. The twist at the end is he removes a bottle of Pepsi from a vending machine at the end of the film.

Product/brand integration is about integrating your product with another entity, which can create a great impact on consumers' minds. Remember that positioning your product is all about positioning it in the minds of the BUYERS!

Retain Existing Customers

Retaining customers is just as important as gaining new ones, and in many ways it is easier to retain prior customers than it is to get new ones. First of all, you know that something about your product and your website appealed to the previous customer. Second, especially if a customer has bought from you more than twice, this customer has a proclivity to the product. Repeat customers are important in any business; you can maintain your revenue just by keeping previous customers happy. In my business, I usually entice existing customers with customer-only sales and other perks.

Even though online retail lacks human interaction, there will still be times when a customer e-mails or telephones your business with a question or a special request. Having an excellent customer service policy promotes goodwill to your customers. Always be polite and courteous in your dealings with customers and they will come back. Even low prices and great merchandise are unlikely to retain customers if you are not courteous to them. Always respond to customer e-mails in a timely manner, and be accommodating to their requests when you can. The competition out there is tough, and keeping your current customers away from the competition is part of your marketing strategy. Here are some tips for retaining current customers:

- Have customer-only sales
- Provide loyal customers with special discounts
- Offer extra perks such as free delivery
- Provide excellent customer service

Marketing through Your Website

I consider my website to be a breeding ground to attract new buyers. It is also the means to retain previous customers. The Internet provides shopping convenience, but the brick-and-mortar store is better able to communicate to the buyers' sensory perception. Buyers can see, smell, touch, and even listen to the product. If they are buying jewelry, they can see the product. If buying perfume, they can smell it. If buying clothing, they can feel the fabric. And if buying a radio or a CD, they can listen to the music.

Unfortunately, you may not have these advantages if you sell exclusively in e-retail. Your website is how you communicate your product, and the strongest sensory perception an online customer can employ when shopping online is the ability to "see" what your website has to offer. While, at first glance, it may seem that a brick-and-mortar store has more advantages, this may not always be the case. Some consumers would rather make purchases online from the comfort of their home. This way they can avoid other shoppers, long check-out lines, and hovering sales clerks. Much of the time customers will find less variety, if not many items out of stock in brick-and-mortar stores. So, a well-designed website that grabs a potential buyer's attention and provides her with excellent and well-informed item descriptions and fantastic photographs can have its advantages. Establishing the buyer's confidence in your site and your product means that your website should communicate pertinent information about the product being offered. This creates a sense of trust from the customer, and it also projects your credibility.

Despite the popularity of online retail, customers tend to be very cautious about buying online, especially if the online store is new and no one has ever heard of it before. As an e-retailer, you have various obstacles in your way to gaining customer trust and loyalty. Today, more and more people are shopping online and there are more e-retailers popping up every day. The competition is tough, and your weapon against the competition is having a great-looking website with great content. Search engine optimization (keyword placement, link campaigns, and pertinent content) helps your search rankings. Good product descriptions and professional-looking photos enhance the credibility of your website. You can take the photos and write the content yourself, but if you have the budget for it, hire a professional photographer and a website copywriter. The message you put on your website also creates the tone of your business and it should communicate to your target audience.

Marketing Your Product

Marketing your product can be done by building awareness of your website, developing good customer service, and finding every opportunity to place your product in the public light. I mentioned earlier that search engine optimization increases your ranking in a search engine result. If you increase the potential customer's chance of accessing your site, then you increase your product's visibility. Make sure that your product descriptions are interesting and that they accurately represent the product. Product description and product picture are important selling points for your product. A clearly written description and a professional-looking product photo convey the message that your site is a serious online retail business, not just some mom-and-pop website. Just because you start out small doesn't mean you have to look small when it comes to your website and how your website presents the merchandise.

(Though there is nothing wrong with selling as a hobby or just to clear out your own personal items that you no longer want. This kind of selling will invariably be done via a shared venue selling site, such as eBay, Etsy, or Addoway. There are many buyers out there who purchase from casual sellers. If you are a casual seller and you cannot afford all the bells and whistles described throughout this book, that is okay. You can still be successful at the level you choose. Again, while this book describes maximum ways to build your business or your own website, each online seller is different. Take from this book what you need for the level of selling you plan to do.)

By providing an excellent return and exchange policy, you are telling the customer that you have the utmost confidence in the quality of your product. At Pearl Paradise.com, we offer a ninety-day guarantee on all of our products. There really aren't any offline jewelry stores that are able to give such a guarantee.

Building product awareness can also be done online and offline. You can donate products to high-profile charity auctions and events, or you can do a promotional campaign through your site stating that a certain portion of the sale will be donated to a particular charity. Product/brand integration is an important part of my marketing campaign for PearlParadise.com. We have participated in the Academy Awards gift basket for three years in a row because it brings an enormous amount of publicity to our product.

Marketing Yourself

Believe it or not, selling your product is selling yourself. How do you sell yourself? Well, you can first become an authority on the product(s) you are selling, then you can let people know about your knowledge. You can write various articles on your website about your product or about things related to your product. You can also get your articles published on different online sites as well as maintain your own blog. If you feel that you may not be a good writer, then you can give workshops or seminars about your product.

In my case, I knew that I had to know all about pearls, so I studied and eventually received a degree from the GIA (Gemological Institute of America). I did this because I needed to know more about the jewelry business, and I knew that it would give me the credibility I needed if I ever had to speak about my product. In the past few years, I've received a lot of press because of my online success. Sometimes the articles just talk about me, and sometimes they are actual interviews. When I'm being interviewed I know that I have to be articulate and interesting because that creates interest in my product. The more press I get, the more exposure PearlParadise.com gets. I am the best spokesperson for my product simply because no one knows pearls the way I do—especially from an online retail standpoint.

You might think that it's difficult to market yourself, but as an entrepreneur, you are the business, and everything that happens to the business will have a direct connection to you.

Public Relations

Public relations is the building of relationships between your business and its target market. In online retail, your target audience can be categorized in four ways: buyer, user, new customer, and existing customer. The way you present the business through your website is one part of your public relations strategy. What kind of relationship do you want to establish with your market? The relationship you build should be a lifelong relationship between you, your customer base, and your potential customers. Public relations involves the way you treat your customers, the way you communicate to them, and the way you present your product to them. You can empower your customers by asking for their opinion on how you can better serve them. You can also associate your business with a nonprofit organization to establish goodwill. Regardless of how you attempt to improve your relationship with your target customer, make sure that the message you send to the public is always favorable. A good public relations campaign will garner product/brand awareness in a favorable light.

Promotions

Marketing is the promotion of any aspect of your business you wish to draw attention to. I must emphasize that a good promotional campaign will do wonders for your business. This is where you can tap into your creativity in devising campaigns that will entice potential buyers. Customer-only promotions are a good way to keep your existing customers happy and loyal. The enormous competition of online retail warrants that you keep your customers interested in your site. They will not buy from the competition if they are constantly buying from you.

I mentioned earlier that at PearlParadise.com we have what I call the "customer-only sale." We offer this to previous customers only (we track this through their buying history). During my numerous visits to Asia, I will buy certain types of pearls that I will only offer to certain customers. I sell these pearls to them nearly at cost, and the product is usually limited to one per customer. This promotion is offered twice a year, and the customers are notified of the sale via e-mail. They are then given a link to a special web page designed specifically for the promotion. The sale is offered on a limited-time basis; we usually allow the sale to go on for a couple of hours. The sales total between $100,000 and $125,000, and although we offer the pearls nearly at cost, the customers usually end up buying other items from our site. The purpose of this promotion is to remind our existing customers of the site, and the tremendous success of this promotion has increased our sales. Keep in mind that this is designed to promote the website, not a particular product.

Another successful promotional campaign was the distribution of our documentary DVD. In 2005 I shot a documentary about one of my pearl-buying trips to China. We sent the documentary to 4,000 of our past customers just before the holiday season. The inclusion of that documentary was the only advertising we did that year. We gave it to existing customers as a way to educate them further about the site and about pearls. A big portion of our business is from return customers, and the pearl video served as a bonus that customers received for making their purchase with us. The DVD created word-of-mouth buzz about the business and it reinforced my credibility as a pearl expert.

You can actually have fun with your promotions as you devise creative promotional campaigns. Although there is some investment involved, you will gain it back in sales. After the release of the pearl video, we had an increase in return customers.

Media Planning

In the beginning I didn't think that I would ever receive the amount of media attention that I've been given. The amount of press that's come my way has been priceless, but it does not last forever. At some point you will have to pay to get yourself in the public eye. Nevertheless, you can get attention by way of press releases, and sometimes they don't cost anything. If you are planning a local event to promote your business, you can contact your local news station, and if the promotion is in conjunction with a charity event, chances are that the station will mention the event to its viewers.

The Four Points of a Press Release

In writing a press release, remember the 4 Ws (who, what, when, and why) and keep the release short and informative.

1. Have a great caption
2. Keep the release to one page
3. Create interest
4. You can submit press releases to an online service such as www.prweb.com or to your local paper and/or news station

10 Tips for Online Retail Marketing

1. Conduct market research
2. Optimize your website
3. Understand the shopping behavior of customers
4. Create a website that is conducive to the taste of your target customers
5. Do not send mass e-mails to promote your business—people will construe this as spam
6. Market your website, your product, and yourself
7. Know the competition
8. Determine the user and the buyer of your product
9. Create a campaign that is conducive to your type of business
10. Think outside the box!

Putting It All Together

Savvy marketing is the reason for my success. Despite all the favorable media attention I've received, none of that would have made any difference if I didn't know how to capitalize on the attention. Marketing is like being an orchestra conductor. You have to guide the various elements to make sure that they are in harmony. There are so many aspects of marketing in business, and to do one without the other is like playing baseball without the ball, or playing basketball without a point guard. You should have some fun designing a marketing campaign for your particular type of online business. But whatever you do, be creative, be aware, and most of all, be passionate about what you are doing.

09

Social Media

We live in a world where if you want to have a viable Internet presence you must learn how to utilize social media sites to your best advantage. If you are not already familiar with social media, I am referring to sites such as Facebook.com, Twitter.com, YouTube.com, as well as blogs, which are necessary elements to your success with an e-commerce business. While there are many other social media sites available for use today with many more constantly being created, for purposes of this book, I will focus only on Twitter, Facebook, YouTube, as well as personal blogs, as these sites are the most widely known and used social media sites today. In other words, if you are going to advertise or market your business and products online, utilizing these sites is essential.

Defining Social Media

Wikipedia defines social media as "media for social interaction, using highly accessible and scalable communication techniques. Social media is the use of web-based and mobile technologies to turn communication into interactive dialogue....Businesses also refer to social media as consumer-generated media (CGM). A common thread running through all definitions of social media is a blending of technology and social interaction for the co-creation of value."

Twitter

Twitter.com allows users to post "tweets," i.e. messages, thoughts, ideas, news, marketing phrases, in short "bursts"—only 140 characters is allowed per tweet (so use your tweet wisely!). You must set up a profile page on Twitter, whereby you will choose a username, which should generally reflect either your business name or the types of products you sell. Your tweets will be displayed on your profile page as well as be seen in the stream of your Twitter "followers." It can be a bit difficult understanding how Twitter works at first, so don't be surprised if it takes you several weeks, or even months, to fully get the hang of it. It also takes time on Twitter to build up a viable and substantial follower base, so you must be patient and continue to work at it. It is important on Twitter as a retailer that you do not tweet your items too often, as that will likely be considered "spam" and you may find that you will quickly lose followers. On Twitter you must learn a delicate balance of marketing, sharing interesting stories, retweeting others' tweets, and communicating with other Twitter users. Twitter commonly uses what are known as "hashtags," whereby a simple search of the hashtag (i.e. #clothes, #shopping) will bring up all tweets using those hashtags (including your own) and are a great way to follow certain topics or participate in communications that interest you and other users.

Expert Tip

I love Twitter. It contains a plethora of information which typically "breaks" on Twitter before any place else. I get the majority of my news and current legislative and legal decisions from those I follow—mostly news organizations, journalists, government entities, and other lawyers.

You can follow me on Twitter at: http://twitter.com/Nicole1515

I'll follow you back!

Facebook

Facebook is a social networking site that allows users to connect with friends, share photographs, link to other sites, and make comments, among many other things. Facebook affords a fabulous platform to showcase your business and, in my opinion, it is essential that most businesses have a Facebook page. I have a Facebook page for all of my businesses. Facebook is a great way to let your customers know when you are having sales, offering special promotions, listing new inventory, or giving general advice or information about products or services. The great thing about a Facebook page for your business is that it allows your customers to interact directly with you and other fans of your business. If a customer has a wonderful experience shopping with you, she is likely to post about her experience on your page, which will be visible to the public.

"I have found that participating actively on Facebook and Twitter are very easy ways to get traffic to your website. With Twitter and Facebook you can come into contact with local customers as well as customers across the globe. I have joined in several groups on Facebook which share all its members' links. Each member will post one of the items he is selling and then pick several other members' items each day to share with friends or fans, and this exposes the items to many more people than just your own friends or fans. This has brought a lot of activity to my eBay store."

—*Kathy Leonard*, eBay ID: kathy188, Store Name: Fancy Pantz Vintage, http://stores.ebay.com/fancy-pantz-vintage

Facebook Fan Pages

Many of you probably already have a personal Facebook page that you use to communicate and share photos with friends and family. If you have an online store (or any business) you should create a separate Facebook "fan" page for your business which could be "liked" (as opposed to "friending" someone on your personal page) by any Facebook member who has an interest in your products.

Marketing on Facebook via a fan page rather than through your personal page is desirable for many reasons. First, your friends and family members will likely get annoyed if their Facebook feed is cluttered up with too many unwanted promotional posts; second, only people who are your "friends" (as opposed to the general public) will see your posts in their feed; third, Facebook limits a "friend" page to only 5,000 friends, so if you wish to have more than 5,000 followers of your business one day, then a fan page is the way to go.

Setting up a fan page just for your business is very simple. If you already have a personal Facebook account, scroll down to the bottom of your profile page and you will see a link called "Create a Page." Click on that, and afterwards you will be prompted with very easy instructions for setting up your page. Your Facebook fan page should be exclusively dedicated to the promotion of your business—in other words, your fan page is not the place to post about what your dog ate for dinner or what a good (or bad) day you had. Of course you will have to spread the word that you have a fan page and this is where friends and family can help you get started—by posting about your new fan page to their friends and family and those that are interested can "like" your page. In order to generate a larger fan base that will likely convert to customers, it is probably necessary that you take out a Facebook ad, which does cost some money, but you can spend only what you choose to and run your ad for as long or short a time as you want.

Facebook Ads

A Facebook Ad is truly an incredible and affordable marketing tool. I have purchased several Facebook Ads and each time met with success. Facebook Ads are simple to create. Again, Facebook will easily prompt you through the steps necessary to generate an ad. The beauty of the Facebook ad is that it can target the specific demographics that you desire worldwide. You can set up a daily budget that you can afford, and you can adjust the amount or end the ad at any time.

"Addoway.com was and is being built on word of mouth. We started off with our own Twitter page and discussed e-commerce and social media and the bridging of the two. We wanted to be experts on the subject and over time we built relationships. We didn't sell anything about Addoway for a long time. The great thing about social media tools like Facebook and Twitter is that you can reach a massive scale of people without spending anything more than just some quality time building your brand. Social media helps you build trust and over time people will want to know what you are a part of. The ROI (return on investment) in social media is always there, you just have to be willing to look in the right places."

—*Fredrick Nijm, CEO and Co-Founder* of Addoway.com

YouTube

YouTube.com is a site that allows users to post videos online. Creating a video advertisement for your online store is another creative way to market your products and your business. The great thing about YouTube is that it is a platform for anybody with an Internet connection to upload videos that can reach a worldwide audience.

YouTube functions similar to other social media sites such as Facebook and Twitter in that you must first create an account before you can upload videos. After you create an account you can start uploading your videos. The tricky part is getting people to view them. People do not need to have an account with YouTube to watch videos, however, people who do create accounts on YouTube are called "subscribers." Subscribers are integral to YouTube success as they are the ones who can give you feedback, rate your videos, and help your videos gain popularity. Gaining subscribers on YouTube takes a bit more work than finding followers on Twitter or fans on Facebook.

Once you have set up a YouTube account you should become involved in the YouTube community. That means watching other people's videos, rating them, and interacting with them—the "social" aspect. When you start forming relationships on YouTube and perhaps collaborating with other subscribers you should begin to notice that larger numbers of people are finding and viewing your videos.

YouTube History

Wikipedia states that "YouTube is a video-sharing website on which users can upload, share, and view videos, created by three former PayPal employees in February 2005…Unregistered users may watch videos, and registered users may upload an unlimited number of videos…In November 2006, YouTube, LLC was bought by Google Inc. for $1.65 billion, and now operates as a subsidiary of Google…According to data published by market research company comScore, YouTube is the dominant provider of online video in the United States, with a market share of around 43 percent and more than 14 billion videos viewed in May 2010."

While marketing your products via YouTube videos can be a great idea, it is vital that you advertise your company in other ways as well, such as through Facebook and Twitter, as it is more difficult to find marketing success on a video-sharing site such as YouTube. YouTube should be used as part of your entire marketing scheme. As you learn more about how various social media sites work, you will begin to get better at marketing through them. Just like with anything else, research and knowledge are key.

Blogs

Another way to spread the word about your business is by creating and maintaining your own blog site. A web log (known as a "blog") is a way for you to write lengthy commentary about your products and business (as opposed to Facebook or Twitter) where comments must generally be kept short. A blog is a particularly good tool to employ for your business as it affords you an opportunity to disseminate information to the public. In other words, whereby on Twitter and Facebook, you will likely be posting links to listings (items you are selling), a blog allows you to write your own stories about your business itself, about the products you sell, about new developments in the industry you are a part of, etc.

You can also gain a large following for your blog if you regularly share updated, useful information with the public. A blog can provide incredible opportunities for interaction with your customers and potential customers. It can help to form a community around your business. In addition, blogs are great ways to build backlinks to your website that are key to gaining higher rankings by search engines.

Blogs are terrific platforms through which to communicate your business expertise and knowledge. The content of your blog can and should be written from a more personal standpoint, rather than the standard traditional marketing style.

Defining Backlinks

According to Wikipedia "Backlinks are incoming links to a website or web page...
Their significance lies in search engine optimization (SEO). The number of backlinks is one indication of the popularity or importance of that website or page (for example, this is used by Google to determine the PageRank of a webpage)."

Blog posts can be composed from many genres of media, including prose, photographs, video, audio, graphs charts—whichever method gets your point across best and has the strongest means by which to gather and keep an audience. For example, if you sell shoes, you can write a blog about the latest fashion trends, or post interesting photos with your own commentary on a celebrity's latest footwear. The point: You can keep your readers entertained as well as directly market your business. A good marketer will appeal to the desires of the customers and keep them interested and coming back for more.

Linking Your Social Media Sites

Now that we have discussed some of the most popular social media sites, you should be aware that in order to maximize their effectiveness you could and you should learn how to use them together. If you have more than one social media account that you use to promote your products, such as Facebook account and a Twitter account, you can use them together by linking them. "Linking" means that you can post a message from your Twitter account and have it appear on your Facebook page automatically and vice versa. This saves you the time and trouble of having to post the same thing more than once.

Social Media Lingo

Here are some useful definitions of the social media lingo you just read about and may not yet be familiar with:

Facebook Feed: A Facebook Feed, also called News Feed is a constant list of updates collected from the user's list of friends' profile pages and featured on the user's home page upon signing in to Facebook. —*firstpagesage.com*

Facebook Friend Page versus Facebook Fan Page: A Facebook Public Profile (also known as Facebook Fan Pages) are special profiles meant to promote a brand, a product, an artist, a website, an organization. Everything public, of course. So, if you want to promote something, you should create a public profile instead of a personal profile. They're very similar: like personal profiles, for example, they have the ability to post status updates (useful to promote your blog posts, for example, since every fan is able to see them directly in their news feeds). You don't need to add fans as friends. —*mycomputermadesimple.blogspot.com*

Facebook Like: A button placed on websites and blogs that Facebook members can click to share their interest in a site with their friends. A Like Box can also be added to a web page that provides a scrolling window into the organization's Facebook Page. The Like Button and Like Box are called "social plugins." —*pcmag.com*

Follower: On Twitter, blogs, and other social media sites, a follower is someone who subscribes to and receives your updates. —*wepopedia.com*

Hashtag: The # symbol, called a hashtag, is used to mark keywords or topics in a Tweet. It was created organically by Twitter users as a way to categorize messages. —*Twitter.com, http://support.twitter.com/entries/49309-what-are-hashtags-symbols*

Retweet: To repost another user's message on the social networking website Twitter. —*en.wiktionary.org*

Spam: Twitter has several definitions of spam. Of importance is: If your updates consist mainly of links and not personal updates. / The list in its entirety can be found here: —*Twitter.com http://support.twitter.com/entries/18311-the-twitter-rules*

Tweeps: 1. A person with a mutual following on www.twitter.com. 2. Conjunction of Twitter and Peeps resulting in tweeps, is commonly used to refer to the Twitter followers of someone. —*urbandictionary.com*

Tweet: 1. A post on Twitter. 2. To post a writing on Twitter.

There are many applications available for use on social media sites that can help you tailor your use of these sites. One such application that Facebook offers is called "Selective Tweets." With Selective Tweets you can update your Facebook status through Twitter, however, you do not have to have every single Tweet appear on your Facebook page. You can choose which tweets you want to post to Facebook—just end a tweet with the hashtag #fb when you want it to post to your Facebook page.

There is a lot of information available on the Internet about how to use these social media sites, and how to use them together. Remember, you must spend time learning and practicing on these sites in order to use them to your full advantage. Just like you must spend time continuing to gain knowledge and experience about your business, you must put the time into learning and understanding the functionality and etiquette of social media sites.

> "**We're living at a time when attention is the new currency:** With hundreds of TV channels, billions of websites, podcasts, radio shows, music downloads, and social networking, our attention is more fragmented than ever before. Those who insert themselves into as many channels as possible look set to capture the most value. They'll be the richest, the most successful, the most connected, capable, and influential among us. We're all publishers now, and the more we publish, the more valuable connections we'll make. Twitter, Facebook, Flickr, Foursquare, Fitbit, and the SenseCam give us a simple choice: participate or fade into a lonely obscurity."
>
> —*Pete Cashmore, CEO* of Mashable

10

Getting Paid

So you have found a product to sell, and you know how you will go about selling it, but how do you get paid? Unlike a brick-and-mortar store that deals with a lot of cash, a reputable online retail business does not accept cash from customers. Accepting cash is just not standard e-retail practice. Besides, most customers will not send cash through the mail, and checks take too long to clear. People shop online because it is easier than going to a store, so paying for their product should be just as easy.

Merchant Account

When I started my business in 1996, I took orders and processed payments over the phone. The customer usually called to place their order and to provide their credit card information. Today, it is much easier for the customer because everything is done electronically. Online retailers cannot productively and profitably exist without accepting credit cards to process customer payments. To do this, a business owner needs to open a merchant credit card account. A merchant credit card account specifically functions to accept credit card payments. There are banks and various independent sales organizations (ISO) that provide merchant credit card processing; they are called merchant account providers (MAP). Unlike a typical business checking account, a merchant account has stricter rules to protect both the merchant and the buyer from credit card fraud. This type of protection is not provided by a regular checking account. When you sign up for an account with a bank or an ISO, you will be able to accept credit cards from your customers. Merchant account providers charge various fees and rates, which depend on the nature, financial status, credit rating, and length of operation of the business.

Choosing the right merchant account provider for your business is one of the most important decisions you will make. Since making a profit is a primary goal in business, your merchant account provider should be cost-efficient for you, as well as convenient and safe for your customer. Banks have stricter rules for merchant credit card accounts, but there are various ISOs out there willing to sign a business owner with a merchant credit card account. Make sure you're cautious and do your research—choosing the right ISO should be approached slowly and methodically. Many businesses make the mistake of not doing enough research on merchant credit card account providers. As a result, these businesses choose a provider that is counterproductive to the growth of their business. The philosophy of a successful online business is to maximize profits by getting the best rates in the various expenditures required to run the online business. To get the best deal for your business, be sure to compare the various rates and fees of merchant account providers. Each provider has its advantages and disadvantages, but it is important that you know what to expect in order to make the right decision for your business—credit card acceptance can make or break an online retail business.

As a business owner, consider the present state of your company's needs, monthly sales, product markup, and potential growth. Banks and merchant account services have their advantages and disadvantages, and the provider you choose should meet the current needs and capability of your business. Most of all, a MAP should give you a cost-efficient plan that will suit your business.

Credit Cards

Accepting credit card payments not only increases the sales of an online business, it also gives credibility to the online business. Online retail has been around for over a decade, and online shoppers are impulsive but savvy. If you have an online retail store that does not provide a secure website to process a customer's credit card transaction, a customer can easily click out of your site. If your site does not accept certain credit cards, your business can lose thousands of dollars in sales. Cashier's checks and money orders are inconvenient for customers (unless they do not have a credit card; but remember that most online purchases are made by people who own credit cards). Alternative forms of payment can be an inconvenience to some buyers, and online shoppers are all about convenience. Credit cards such as Master-Card, Visa, American Express, and Discover are the most frequently accepted cards by online businesses. Businesses can accept MasterCard and Visa by simply signing up with a MAP, but American Express and Discover provide a merchant service to their customers. The most common credit cards accepted by online businesses are MasterCard and Visa, but as your business grows, it is wise to give your customers more credit card options. You can give your customers the added option of making a payment through PayPal or electronic checks.

How an Online Transaction Works

The process of an online transaction is similar to that of a brick-and-mortar store transaction. Shopping in the real world involves the following: a customer chooses a product, the product is put in a shopping cart, and a sales clerk processes the payment transaction. A credit card is usually swiped in a machine, approval is given, and a process takes the funds from the credit card company to the merchant's credit card account. After a specified amount of time, the provider transfers the funds to the merchant's credit card account.

Instead of the person-to-person transaction, online transactions are done virtually, but the process is somewhat the same. In an online transaction, the buyer chooses the item to buy, it is put in a shopping cart, the buyer inputs the necessary information (address and credit card information), approval is given, and it is just a matter of moments before the transaction is complete.

There are two elements involved in processing an online transaction:

- The Internet merchant credit card account
- The payment gateway account (the online card processor)

These are separate components, each with a different function, but both are needed to accept credit card transactions. The merchant credit card account is a special account just for credit card acceptance. Think of the merchant credit card account as being similar to a cash register; it is where the funds are kept before the funds are deposited to the merchant's bank account. The payment gateway account, on the other hand, is like a sales counter in the real world. In a brick-and-mortar store, the customer places the merchandise on a counter where a salesperson processes the transaction. The gateway, in essence, does the processing of the credit card. The following is an example of a standard online transaction process:

- The buyer chooses an item(s) to purchase.
- The buyer inputs his/her information on a secure website.

- The total order is put together by a shopping cart program that adds the total purchase, including tax and shipping, then prepares the total amount for credit card processing.
- The information is transmitted to the payment gateway by the shopping cart program.
- The payment gateway checks the status of the credit card.
- If the card is accepted by the customer's credit card company, the credit card company sends that information back to the payment gateway. If the credit card is denied, the gateway program asks the buyer to provide another credit card or the transaction cannot be completed.
- Once the credit card is accepted for the total amount of purchase, this information is sent to the merchant, thus confirming the order.

Whew! And all this occurs within moments. Once the customer types in his/her credit information, approval or denial happens immediately. Then the following process takes place:

- The funds are transferred to and held by the merchant account provider's account for a specified period of time.
- The amount is then scheduled for transfer to the merchant's bank account.

Payment Gateway

A payment gateway is a program that processes the credit card information of a buyer. It encrypts the customer's credit card information to make sure that the transaction is secure during the process of transaction. The program delivers the credit card information to and from the card provider and to the merchant. Gateways are like messengers delivering top-secret information that is written in code. Payment gateways help prevent credit card fraud by determining the consistency of the billing address with the address of the purchaser. The following are the most commonly used payment gateways:

- PayPal.com
- Google Checkout

Some online merchant credit card providers will have a payment gateway as part of their service, but the fees will vary with each provider.

Evaluating Your Business

Now that you have a basic idea about how an online transaction works and the two important components in processing a sales transaction, evaluating your businesses is the next step in being able to choose the right MAP for your business. Before beginning to shop around for a merchant credit card account provider, evaluate the current situation of your business. Businesses selling low-cost items should study their markup to make sure that the various fees involved in acquiring a MAP do not eat up all the profit. How your business qualifies for a merchant credit card account depends on the following:

- The length of time you've been in business.
- Your credit rating.
- Nature of product sold.
- Geographical location of the business. (Although online, the business must be physically located in the United States. Businesses not located in the United States cannot obtain a US merchant bank account. WorldPay.com is an alternative for foreign businesses.)

Start-up businesses might find it hard to qualify for a merchant credit card account with a bank, but there are companies out there willing to work with newly established online businesses. Just be aware of their extra fees and costs. Assess your current financial situation and the financial situation of your business or corporation. You should ask yourself the following questions:

- How much can I mark up my product price to cover overhead and the costs of transacting online and still remain price competitive?

- What is my credit rating?
- Is my business considered high-risk?

There are also two important things to consider when choosing the right MAP service: real-time processing (automated transaction processing) and the technical compatibility of the MAP with your e-commerce system.

Real-time processing automatically checks the validity of the customer's credit card, and once the card is accepted, the information is sent back to your website. The funds are eventually deposited into your business's checking account. Automated transaction processing is quick and convenient for the customer, but it is more expensive for the retailer. Established businesses with high sales transactions usually opt for real-time processing. On the other hand, manual processing collects the information the customer types into your buy site, and you then process the information manually. When I first began, I used manual processing, but as my sales grew, it was no longer efficient. Nevertheless, manual processing is cheaper than automated transaction processing. New businesses with low sales volume usually choose to process payments manually. Businesses making custom-made merchandise (due to its long lead time) also opt for manual processing. However, if you offer overnight or next-day shipping for your customers once the product is purchased, you might find yourself burning the midnight oil manually inputting the customer's information and having to do credit card checks.

Another issue to consider is technical compatibility. A merchant account provider's hosting system, a program that allows transmission of a website, might not be compatible with your hosting system. It is similar to renting a space in the brick-and-mortar world. The servers charge a monthly fee for the service. Individuals with Internet connection can act as servers or hosts, but most online companies choose professional web hosting companies for the following reasons:

- It is cheaper than running your own server.
- Hosting companies provide a service for backing up your files.
- It offers twenty-four-hour monitoring of your site.
- It provides uninterrupted connection to the Internet.

Professional hosting is more convenient than having to worry about keeping up your own website. However, there are various hosting systems out there, so make sure that your hosting system is compatible with the hosting system of the online merchant credit card account provider you choose.

Banks

Most businesses will open a business account with a bank, and this usually entails a checking account with the name of the business or corporation, or a DBA if the merchant is a sole proprietor. But a home-based online retail business will also need to open a merchant credit card account with a bank or an independent sales organization that advertises on the WWW. Establishing a merchant account can be difficult for a small, newly formed business. Most banks will do a credit check and require some sort of financial statement from the business. However, banks tend to prefer to do business with already established companies, and they also prefer brick-and-mortar businesses. Nevertheless, if you have been doing business in your bank for a while and you know the people, talk to your bank representative about opening a merchant credit card account and ask about the requirements.

Pros

- Familiarity with the establishment (you know the bank and you know the people).
- Bank rates can be cheaper for already established businesses.

Cons

- Banks tend to turn down online businesses.
- The application process can be complicated.
- Bank rates can run high for start-up businesses.

Independent Sales Organizations (ISO)

There are various independent sales organizations that provide merchant credit card accounts. An ISO is not a bank but a service that basically conducts the required credit check to see if a merchant qualifies for an online merchant credit card account. Although ISOs are friendlier than banks when it comes to dealing with online businesses and the application process is not as complex, the online merchant still has to qualify for the account. Small businesses usually opt to go with an ISO rather than a local bank because ISOs are not as stringent with the qualification process. Think of ISOs as brokers, and while their fees and rates might tend to be a bit higher than a bank's, they are usually eager to obtain the accounts of online businesses. Signing up with an ISO means that after a sale is made, the funds from a customer's credit card account go to the ISO's account; the funds are eventually transferred to the merchant's bank account.

Pros

- ISOs can offer home-based online businesses competitive rates, along with other perks.
- It is easier to qualify with an ISO than with a bank.
- The application process is less complicated.

Cons

- Because an ISO is a broker of sorts, they can add various fees and costs to your contract.

Third-Party Merchant Account Providers

A third-party merchant account provider already has an existing merchant credit card account that they allow online merchants to use. Merchants with bad credit, newly formed online businesses, and offshore online businesses have better luck with third-party providers than with banks or ISOs. Third-party merchant account providers tend to be more expensive than banks or ISOs because third-party providers actually have to pay a merchant account provider. Nevertheless, a third-party provider may be a short-term solution for a newly formed or high-risk home-based online business until the business establishes itself financially. Companies such as PayPal and 2Checkout.com are third-party providers.

When making an online payment, the buyer is redirected to the third-party provider's website to complete the transaction. The transaction is processed under the name of the third-party merchant account provider. In essence, businesses using third-party providers become drop shippers, and the third-party provider becomes the seller. Some credit card companies such as MasterCard and Visa do not allow third-party providers to process their transactions.

Pros

- Easier for businesses to qualify with a third-party provider.
- Length of time you've been in business is less of an issue than it is with banks.
- Some do not require start-up or monthly fees.

Cons

- Higher processing fees and costs.
- Fund transfers take longer compared to banks and ISOs.
- Decreases credibility of an online retail business.

Rates and Fees

You want to be in business to make a profit, and the rates and fees of a bank, ISO, or third-party merchant account provider should be able to work with your business so that you are still able to make a reasonable profit despite the various charges. Obtaining a merchant credit card processing account with a bank, ISO, or third-party provider is a key factor in a home-based online retail business, so it is important that you know what you are in for. Obtaining a merchant credit card account consists of the following: one-time fees, fixed monthly fees, and variable monthly fees.

- **One-Time Fee:** This payment is for the application and gateway fee. Beware of ISOs without application fees because some will just pad up the payment gateway fee. Some merchant account application fees are not refundable, even if the business is declined an account, so make sure that you ask your representative about this cost.
- **Fixed Monthly Fees:** These fees are charged to your account every month by the gateway provider, and the amount stays the same. The fees are the same each month, and they usually cover payment cancellations and transaction reports.
- **Variable Monthly Fees:** This fee fluctuates from month to month depending on the amount of your sales. The variable monthly fee involves the following: transaction fees, discount rates (do not let the name fool you), charge-back rates, and charge-back fees.

Qualifying for a Merchant Credit Card Account

What is your credit rating? The average rating is approximately 692 (as of January 2011), but if your credit rating falls below this number, you might be considered a high-risk business if you are a single proprietor. Qualifying for a merchant credit card account is similar to applying for a credit card. High-risk businesses, such as online retail stores selling adult-themed products, might find it difficult to qualify for a merchant credit card account. Businesses outside of the United States are required to have a merchant account with a US bank and a website server located in the United States.

Breakdown of Variable Monthly Rate and Fees:

- **Transaction fees** are the fixed charges on every sale transaction that your online business makes. Hint: If you are selling low-cost items such as CDs, DVDs, or books, a high transaction fee can hurt your business.

- **Discount fees** are nonfixed charges. A percentage is taken from every sale that your business transacts. The fee is charged by the credit card company and the merchant account provider. Your contract might stipulate a minimum discount fee charge, which means that, for example, if your minimum discount fee charge is $25 and your total discount fee is only $20, you are still responsible for paying the $25. Hint: If you are selling high-cost items, it is better to have a higher transaction fee and a lower discount fee.

- **Refund rates** are for returned items that are charged back to your account. Do not go with a merchant credit account provider that charges a refund rate.

- **Charge-back fees** occur when a customer orders a charge-back from the credit card company because the customer did not actually purchase an item. This usually occurs as a result of credit card fraud when a credit card holder finds out that another party has used his/her charge card to buy products online. Charge-backs are similar to bounced checks and they can hurt your credit rating.

Alternative Forms of Payment

Although credit cards are the most frequently used forms of payment for online purchases, there are other alternatives available.

- **Internet Checks:** Customers using this type of payment will enter their bank account information into a secure website. The funds are transferred from the customer's checking account to the merchant's account. The transfer usually takes between ten and fourteen days. It is advisable for merchants to use check-guaranteed services when using this type of payment acceptance.
- **Money Orders/Cashier's Checks:** This is a convenient alternative for customers who do not have credit cards or checking accounts.
- **Personal Checks:** Merchants will usually wait until the customer's check is cleared before shipping the item.

Now that you know about these alternative forms of payment, remember that a legitimate online business looking to establish credibility in the eyes of customers and lenders will always opt for credit card payments. Credit cards are the most common type of payment, but it is a good idea to give your customers other payment options.

Shopping Around

There are many ISOs and third-party providers out there, and finding the right one for your business means that you will have to do your research. Most providers advertise on the Internet, but not all state their fees. Some companies will have free application fees, but their gateway fee might be exorbitant. Do not get fooled by freebies because providers will just charge you more elsewhere. When you are searching for a provider, get the rates and fees of three to five providers and compare the figures before talking to a company representative. Then consider the nature of your business and determine which services are the most feasible for you. Some providers do not process all credit cards, so find one that at least works with Visa and MasterCard since those two cards are the most frequently used. When talking to an account representative, you should ask and consider the following:

- Get a clear quote of their rates and fees, and get it in writing. Be aware of all charges, rates, and fees. Be cautious of hidden charges.
- What credit limit does your business qualify for?
- How long is the contract?
- What are the incurred fees if you break your contract with the provider?

- How long does it take the provider to transfer the funds to your account? Some take one day, and others can take as long as five days. (Some third-party providers make the deposit at the end of the month, and this can hurt your cash flow.)
- What kind of fringe benefits can they offer? (Some offer discounts on advertising.)
- If your monthly sales suddenly increase, some providers will hold onto the funds because you might have gone over your limit. Ask about their policy for holding over-the-limit funds.
- How long has the provider been in business?
- Who are their customers?

There are many things to consider in your search for a provider. So, when you are shopping around, remember to compare the prices and services of various providers. Tell the account representative that you have done research—most providers are willing to negotiate with you, and some may even match or beat the lower rates of other providers just to get your business. When you talk to a merchant service provider, they will also offer you information on the following:

- Qualified rates and nonqualified rates for MasterCard and Visa
- Monthly minimum fee for MasterCard and Visa
- Monthly wireless fee
- Batch settlement fee

Some like to pad up your bill with extras that you might not need. Find out what type of support they provide and if it is compatible with your support system. Remember that matching the current status of your business with what a credit card account provider has to offer is important. Think of your business and the provider as two pieces of a puzzle.

When your business begins to boom, it might also be time to renegotiate your contract with your provider. Do not continue to pay for old rates and fees, especially if you have the negotiating power. Most providers will negotiate with you just to keep your business if you let them know that you have a better offer from another provider. Always keep your options open. It is a good idea to make a monthly assessment of your business to make sure that the rates and fees remain cost-effective.

Seller Beware

As your business grows and you improve in the search rankings, you will enjoy greater exposure and increased sales. The drawback to this is that as your sales increase, you might not be able to scrutinize every single order the same way you did when you first started out. Although credit card purchases are safe on sites that are protected by a secure payment gateway, there are sites out there that require your credit card information before they allow you to enter the site. This is particularly common in adult-themed websites. The problem is that although most online shoppers are very careful and buy from sites that provide a secure payment transaction, there are still those who unsuspectingly provide their credit card information to sites that are not so secure. Most online credit card fraud occurs because an unsuspecting individual's credit card number has been pulled from a nonsecure site.

Because an online transaction can be done completely anonymously, the merchant has no power to check the ID of the individual making the purchase. This can cause harm to the merchant if the purchase is successful and the credit card number used is a fraudulently obtained number. In this situation the only loser is the merchant.

Do not think that just because you have a secure site, credit card fraud will not happen to you. Your site might be secure, but who is going to protect you from the buyer? Anyone selling a product that is of any value is a target of online credit card fraud. Every year the thieves get a little trickier and more sophisticated, and every year merchants such as myself combat their actions with more security measures. International credit card fraud is especially prevalent, and it keeps online merchants on their toes. In my experience, orders from countries such as Indonesia, Nigeria, and Romania are a constant threat to online merchants.

If a product is purchased from your website with a stolen card, and you ship the product out, you lose the product, the cost of shipping, and your credit rating suffers when the true owner of the credit card realizes that an unauthorized purchase has been made. The victim will simply call their credit card company and dispute the charges. In turn, the credit card company will file a charge-back with your merchant processor, and the previously deposited funds will be removed from your bank account. There is no priority placed on effectively combating this type of credit card fraud because, essentially, the merchant is the only one that loses.

How Increased Sales Cost Me a Fortune

When I first started out in business, there really wasn't a guide out there to warn me about merchant credit card account providers. In 1997 I decided that I finally had to obtain a merchant account provider, so I went with Cardservice International. They had been around for a long time, and I felt that the contract they gave me was reasonable. At the time, my sales were between $10,000–$15,000 a month. In June 2003 *Newsweek* magazine wrote about me and my business in a feature article titled "SARS Special." I was one of the few merchants who trekked out to China during the SARS epidemic. As a result, I was able to buy pearls at extremely low prices, and I was able to develop long-standing relationships with the pearl farmers there. The moment the *Newsweek* article hit the stands, my monthly sales figures skyrocketed from $10,000–$15,000 a month to $100,000 a month. As a result, I went over my credit limit charges, and Cardservice International held onto the funds for five months.

I had been in business for over three years when my accountant finally brought to my attention that the merchant fees I had been paying were too high. Not keeping abreast of the changes in fees and charges, especially as they pertained to my growing business, cost me approximately $50,000. The first company I talked to did a rate comparison. I was shocked by what I found out. They showed me that I had overpaid more than $1,000 in unnecessary fees in just the previous month. They informed me that merchant service providers are more competitive now and some merchant card companies do not even charge a fee for returns. Although my returns were rare, I was paying 2 percent of the total cost of refund, and since I had such a high sales volume and some of my products were high-cost items, it was costing me several hundred dollars per month! Armed with this knowledge, I began shopping around for another provider. I now use Pivotal Payments with Yahoo Search. Pivotal looked at my business in the long-term, and they were able to give me competitive rates and fees, along with perks such as pay-per-click advertising with Yahoo. Today, the money I save amounts to nearly $30,000 per year!

The Lesson Learned:
Always evaluate the current sales of your business and make growth projections. If your business has a strong marketing campaign, or if your business suddenly

receives favorable press from the media, expect an increase in sales and consider renegotiating your contract, or shop around for a new provider. Beware of hidden costs and archaic fees. The e-retail business is new and is changing constantly, and merchant terms are also changing to compete with each other. Knowing this will save you money and much unnecessary frustration.

This is a situation that I have been fighting for years. I do such a great amount of business that it takes the eye of a hawk to detect a suspicious order, but it is possible. The following are examples of the type of fraud that my company battles on a daily basis.

Standard Fraudulent Order

I use the term "standard fraudulent order" in this section to define the most common types of fraudulent orders. Fraudulent orders can come in many forms, because when people want to cheat you, they can come up with the most ingenious ways to "get something for nothing." A standard fraudulent order comes into your system with a standard international shipping destination. The order will typically have a special request attached to it for "the fastest shipping available." Put a red flag on purchasers willing to pay between $50–$100 for shipping. They will also ask you not to indicate the real value of the item because they do not want to pay customs duties (they are stealing the item from you, but they do not want to pay to steal). However, when shipping an item, the value is usually put on the label for insurance purposes. A request to not list the value should be an indication that there is something wrong with the order.

Sometimes fraudulent orders will include other special requests. They might include instructions indicating that the purchase is a gift, and the "purchaser" might request to have the item shipped to a different address.

Standard Fraudulent Order with a Contact

A typical order will come through with an e-mail contact for an individual posing as a store owner overseas. He or she will inquire if you ship internationally and if you accept credit cards. This e-mail should be a red flag. I guarantee that any order you transact from an individual posing to be in this situation is a fraudulent order. I have read hundreds of requests like this since the late 1990s, and all of them have been 100 percent fraudulent.

> **Rule for Checking the Standard Fraudulent Order**
>
> Pay special attention to orders coming from under developed countries. If possible, indicate in your terms and policies the payment method (such as wire transfers) for international orders. Although all countries are suspect when it comes to international credit card fraud, many fraudulent orders of this type have come from the following countries: Nigeria, the Philippines, Indonesia, Romania, and Russia. All of the orders I have ever received from the above-mentioned countries have been from stolen credit cards, and I hope that the situation changes in the immediate future. But, for now, seller beware!

Fraudulent Order with Incorrect Country Code

This is a fairly new method that credit card thieves have concocted. If you shop online, you will see that some e-retailers request that shoppers input their country code when filling in the personal information section of the shopping cart. Not all online retailers do this. Some will just ask shoppers to indicate their country of origin. The way your customers identify their country of origin depends on the shopping cart program you have on your site.

Cheating customers will take advantage of this system by inserting their full address with one small alteration—they will change their own country code to a country code in our "green zone" (a country from which fraudulent orders are not prevalent). The thief is hoping that when the package is shipped, the shipping company will determine that the address is in another country (by checking the postal code and the city name), and that when the package is dispatched it will be re-routed to the correct address.

Fraudulent Order Requesting the Forwarding of Money or Product

This type of order requests that you either receive payments or receive products for another company; your task is to forward either the products or the payments to the company's main office in another country. This is typically sent to you as a type of job offer with a 10 percent (or greater) commission for each transaction. This scam has become especially prevalent in the last couple of years, and the victims accepting these types of payments will soon realize that the bank checks they have received are fraudulently produced. Those receiving products will realize that they have become pawns when the police show up at their door.

As a new business owner, you might think that this is an easy way to make money while you are waiting for your sales to increase. Think again. You might not think that online retailers receive this type of "offer," but they do. In my business, I've encountered this type of request numerous times, and it always seemed weird to me that a stranger would actually contact me with such an offer. Anyone approached with something like this should just BEWARE. Remember, if it sounds too good to be true, it usually is!

Fraudulent Orders with Bogus Checks

Bogus checks and bogus bank orders also present a problem. This is not such a difficult issue to deal with. All you have to do is explain to your bank that you have received payment from a customer for a product and you would like to ensure that the payment is valid before you ship the product. This usually takes the bank about a week. If a customer issues you a check for a larger amount than the total purchase, asks that you take the amount owed you and remit the remainder to them along with the product, this is a scam—a very typical scam.

Customer Trust

Your customers should feel safe when purchasing from your online business because customer security is essential to building your online business reputation and customer base. A potential buyer should feel that they are dealing with a reputable online company that has taken the preventive measures to protect its customers. The biggest challenge of start-up online retail business is ensuring customer trust. One way to ensure customer trust is to join organizations such as the Better Business Bureau (BBB), which offer programs specifically for online businesses. The recognition of a reliable third party on your website can increase sales and lets customers know that your business has met the standards of online ethical practices. The BBB offers two programs for online businesses:

- **Reliability Seal Program:** A seal exclusively for online businesses stating that the online business is a member of the Better Business Bureau, and that the business has met the requirements for meriting the seal.

- **Privacy Seal Program:** A seal exclusively for online businesses stating that the online business has met the requirements of the Better Business Bureau in protecting the privacy of customers' information.

There are requirements for qualifying for the Reliability and Privacy Seal Program. For more information, log on to www.bbb.org.

Another issue concerning customer trust is credit card fraud. Although credit card fraud is not as prevalent online as some might think (in fact, credit card payments are one of the safest ways to pay and receive payment), credit card fraud still happens. Make sure that your merchant provider has an Address Verification Service (AVS) in their system. AVS compares the billing address of the credit card to the records of the bank issuing the card. MasterCard and Visa use the card validation code 2 (CVC2), which asks the customer to type in the three-digit code printed on the back of the card. The risk of fraud is minimal, but if your business sells high-end products, the charge-back rate of disputed merchandise can sting. Analyze your sales and be suspicious of unusually large purchases from a single individual. Make sure you ask the merchant card service representative about this issue.

Last Words

Looking for the right merchant card service provider does not have to be costly if you shop around, but it will take some time. Without a credit card provider and a credit card processor, you cannot secure sales, because most who shop online use credit cards. Running a successful online business means that every aspect of the business is thoroughly researched before a sale even takes place. Try to exercise some patience in this regard. No doubt, you are excited about having a business, but a business hastily put together is like a house built without nails. So make sure that you build your business carefully, safely, and most of all, take the time to find out what you need to know—it will save you money in the long run, and it will help your business succeed.

11 Shipping Methods

Most books about starting your own business probably don't devote a whole chapter to shipping, but in the online retail world, shipping decisions are key to your survival. When you first start out, orders might be relatively small and you might be able to ship orders as they trickle in, but as your business grows and orders increase, you will need to have an organized shipping system. Customers want to receive their product on time and in good condition. Being organized with shipping will save you time, and determining the most efficient and cost-effective way to ship your merchandise will save you money. Many online businesses lose customers and revenue because of lost or damaged products. These types of incidents will happen, but part of your customer service ethic is to minimize the risk of such incidents. Some businesses ship only on certain days of the week, and some ship every day. How you determine your shipping standards will have much to do with the nature of your business and the system that you've incorporated as part of your business operation.

Determining the Best Way to Ship

I generally recommend FedEx or the United States Postal Service (USPS) to handle your shipping needs. These companies have been around a long time, and they are widely used by private individuals and businesses. Each company has its strengths and weaknesses, but what you need to be aware of is that choosing the right shipper for your business is determined by your customers' needs and your own experience with the carrier or carriers that you choose. Moreover, choosing a shipper with an efficient package tracking system can help protect you from customer malfeasance. For example, if a customer claims that a product was never received, you can go on the shipper's website and track the shipment. FedEx, UPS, and USPS provide a tracking system that lets you know when a package was shipped and delivered. You will be amazed at how some people will claim that they never received the merchandise, that the merchandise took too long to arrive, or that the product was damaged when it was received. You can protect yourself better from fickle or "difficult" customers by going with a reliable shipper.

Your website should provide the following shipping information:

- Shipping method: Standard, Priority, Overnight
- Shipping cost
- Optional or nonoptional insurance

Providing adequate shipping information to your customers lets them know their options. One thing to remember is that online shopping might be more convenient for the customers, but the instant gratification is delayed. Customers can't walk out with the product in their hand. Instead, you have to focus on keeping customers informed of the whereabouts of their packages as a means to alleviate the longer wait.

FedEx

I recommend FedEx for high-value items because my experience with them has been good and their tracking methods are very user-friendly. FedEx ships to local, national, and international destinations. When you decide to use FedEx, you will need to call and ask for an account representative. You can log on to www.fedex. com to get more detailed information. You can open an account online or talk to an account representative. I recommend talking to the representative because the FedEx site tends to have too much information, and it can be confusing. Be sure to ask the representative for any available discounts, especially if you decide to use FedEx exclusively. Although they are a big company, there is room for negotiation of fees, and you can also inquire about any additional discounts where they may apply. FedEx tries to remain competitive by offering third-party discounts. PearlParadise .com joined the MJSA (Manufacturers Jewelers of America) because they offer FedEx benefits that saved us thousands of dollars each month. Then I signed up for an American Express card through FedEx because it added an additional 5 percent savings for each shipment.

Pros

- Good for high-value items
- On-time delivery
- Minimal late delivery and package loss
- Efficient tracking system
- On-site package pickup
- Ships worldwide
- Customers can order free shipping supplies (mail tubes, envelopes, and flat-rate boxes) online

Cons

- Higher shipping costs
- Tends to ignore signature confirmations during busy seasons
- Packages occasionally arrive in very poor condition

Regardless of the cons with FedEx, they are still one of the most reliable and one of the safest shipping companies I have used.

History of Federal Express

- The idea for Federal Express was conceived by Frederick W. Smith, a Yale University undergraduate who wrote a term paper on the inefficiency of the passenger route system when it came to delivering time-sensitive materials.

- Smith created the name "Federal Express" because of its patriotic connotation, and his idea that it would attract the public because of its name recognition.

- Federal Express officially became "FedEx" in 1994 as a result of customers using the shorter version of the name.

USPS

Before FedEx, UPS, and other various shipping agencies, there was the United States Postal Service, and over 225 years later, it's still a pretty reliable system. Individuals and businesses alike use USPS for all their shipping needs. As with FedEx, USPS also has an efficient website to help customers with shipping, tracking packages, packing supplies, etc. From postcards to parcels, USPS ships locally, nationally, and worldwide. You can access their website at www.usps.com for a complete listing of their services. USPS is good for medium-priced items. Although their track record for shipping is fairly good, they have lost some of our packages, especially during the holidays when chaos usually permeates the post office.

Pros

- Good for medium-priced items
- More economical than FedEx
- Many locations throughout the United States
- Will not leave packages without signature confirmation. Customers can pick up packages at the nearest post office location.

Cons

- Can lose packages during heavy shipping seasons
- Can be slow

UPS

UPS started as a messenger company in the United States in 1907. Since then it has become a widely used shipping agency with locations throughout the United States, and it is used by both individuals and businesses. They ship everything from letters to oversized packages and provide a fairly efficient package tracking system. Most people are more familiar with UPS than FedEx. Log on to www.ups.com to find out more about their products and services. I find that UPS works for shipping oversized packages because they really focus on packaging and crating oversized packages. You can go to your local UPS store or arrange for package pickup. Remember, however, that you need to call at least a day before your shipping date, and your package must be packed and labeled before the UPS representative arrives at your place of business.

Pros

- Good for large packages
- Cheaper than FedEx
- Will not leave packages without signature confirmation

Cons
- Slower than FedEx
- Tends to lose more packages, in my experience

Stamps.com

Established in 1999 Stamps.com is a service that allows you to print postage, labels, and any other shipping labels you may need from the Stamps.com website. You can print postage and labels on either plain paper or directly on the envelope. There is a $15.99 monthly charge for the basic service, and you have the option to cancel the service at any time. Another great thing about Stamps.com is that the USPS "1-pound rule" doesn't apply. At the post office, if you are shipping a package that weighs over 1 pound, you are required to deliver it in person to an actual postal employee. If you use Stamps.com, this requirement is eliminated, and if you are shipping packages every day, this service can save you hours each week because you won't have to fall in line—you can just drop your packages at the post office and leave. In some areas, USPS offers at-home pick up. Go to usps.com/pickup to see if it's available in yours. Stamps.com also checks the validity of a customer's address. Customers can make mistakes in typing their addresses, and Stamps.com can catch the typo and fix it for you. For more detailed information about their services, log on to www.stamps.com.

Since you'll be starting out as a home-based retail business, you will probably begin by using the "Pro" service, which prints USPS postage and labels and offers a $250 maximum postage balance. You can then graduate to the other options as your business grows.

Proper Packaging

As I mentioned in chapter 7, your website is the introduction of your business to shoppers. Your website showcases your items for sale, and it makes certain promises to the buyer about the product and service that you offer. After the shopper buys and pays for the product, their second experience with your business will be the arrival of the merchandise and the condition of the product when they open the package. The following are a few questions to ask yourself when thinking about how a customer will perceive your business:

- Has the package arrived on time?
- Did the customer receive the correct merchandise?
- Did the merchandise arrive free of damage?

You don't have to be fancy, but a professional-looking label with the name and address of your business gives you the extra credibility that a handwritten note does not. Having labels professionally printed or having a stamp made of your name and address doesn't need to cost much, so long as you don't get too fancy. Also make sure that the customer's address is printed correctly. Double-checking addresses will save you time and money. There is nothing worse for the seller than shipping a package to the wrong address. Also make sure that breakable items have enough cushion or fillers in the box to prevent breakage. It's a rather rude surprise for a customer to receive a box and hear something rattling inside. If this happens, chances are that customer won't buy from you again.

Handling Returns

Business owners never want to handle returns. But a customer-friendly return policy conveys credibility and trust in the eyes of your customers. The idea is that if a customer has the option to return the merchandise, they will feel more confident about buying from you. But chances are good that if a customer is happy with the product, they will keep it.

How I Shipped Orders in the Beginning

When I started selling pearls in 1996, I was a one-man operation. I sold my products online, but everything was done manually. I even took orders on the phone. Orders came via e-mail, and I wrote down the addresses of the customers for my records, then I manually transferred them to shipping labels. I packaged the orders, then I went to USPS and hand-delivered the packages to a postal clerk for processing.

How I Ship Orders Now

Today, I have several employees who process orders. Orders come in through a merchant processing system. The orders are downloaded several times each day, with one copy saved on our server and a hard copy printed as a customer receipt. We then transfer the shipping information from our system to either FedEx or USPS and a shipping label is printed. The shipping label and customer receipt then go to our "fulfillment department," where the orders are filled. The orders are packaged and sealed twice, the proper labels are placed, and they are set aside for pickup.

Note: Your packaging and shipping system will change as your business evolves and as technology changes, but one thing to remember is to always double-check the orders, customer addresses, and shipping labels.

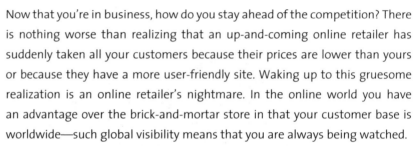

12 | Staying Ahead of the Competition

Now that you're in business, how do you stay ahead of the competition? There is nothing worse than realizing that an up-and-coming online retailer has suddenly taken all your customers because their prices are lower than yours or because they have a more user-friendly site. Waking up to this gruesome realization is an online retailer's nightmare. In the online world you have an advantage over the brick-and-mortar store in that your customer base is worldwide—such global visibility means that you are always being watched.

Being the best on the Net is a constant game. If you do something new, someone will take your idea and try to do it better. This fight to attract the most customers, rank the highest in a search engine result, and close the most sales will keep you on the lookout for the enemy—the competition.

Staying ahead of the competition means that you can never get comfortable in your business. Now, this doesn't mean that you should employ paranoia as a strategy. But you have to understand that having a business is like having a child. It is always growing and evolving, and it must adapt to its current environment in order to survive. Constant improvement is the key to staying on top. In order to stay ahead of the competition, you must constantly think outside the box. You need to come up with original ideas, methods, and strategies that no one else is using.

The irony is that once you employ these methods, someone will take notice and steal them away, and you'll have to devise new ones. That is just the nature of the online world.

Brainstorming

If you're working alone, with partners, or with employees, set aside time for a brainstorming session at least once every other week. My office actually does this every payday. We listen to each other and we try to come up with new ideas and solutions to problems.

If you're brainstorming by yourself, you can list ideas on a piece of paper as you come up with them, or you can cluster your ideas. Try going somewhere you've never been and see if that place inspires your creative juices. If you're brainstorming with a group of people, make sure that you initiate a moderator. The moderator can introduce the issue at hand, and the group members can individually write down their ideas on a sheet of paper, or the moderator can write down the ideas on a chalkboard. After each topic is discussed to everyone's satisfaction, you can proceed to the next brainstorming topic. This activity actually promotes goodwill among employees because it empowers them, and you'll be surprised by the ideas that will come out of the sessions. Below are common brainstorming topics for an online retail business:

- Website improvement
- Marketing plans
- Merchandising
- Pricing
- Conducting effective research
- Product development
- Problem solving
- Advertising
- Project management
- Process management

What is Clustering?

Clustering is the method of grouping similar ideas together.

Always be a critical thinker in assessing your business, and look into where you might be able to improve your prices, your product presentation (website, photography, and description), promotions, product placement, and customer service. Find little areas in your business and website that you can improve upon. Little steps can make a big difference. Researching the Net is critical at this point. Always be aware of your competition and of everything they are doing. You cannot stay ahead of them if you don't know they are creeping up behind you.

I spend a portion of each day in my office examining other pearl jewelry sites. I always know in what direction they are headed, and I always make sure to stay ahead of them. I monitor what they're selling, how they're pricing it, and their customer service policy. Then I determine if they have changed their website in any way. Have they added more links? If so, where are the links coming from and where are they leading to? Are their promotions different, or are they similar to mine? Have they added to their product line? These are the types of questions you should ask when researching other sites. Keep a record of your findings and continue to monitor these sites.

Improving on Your Competitors' Ideas

Tough competition means that you have to get tough as well. I mentioned earlier that there are those who will copy every idea that we come up with at PearlParadise.com. There's nothing we can do about it except come up with new and better ideas. But sometimes you might stumble onto a competitor that has come up with something very original. Do not copy that competitor's ideas—that would be unethical and wrong. What you can do, however, is take the idea and make it better. If a competitor has devised a way to improve the presentation of their pearls, see if you can also improve your product presentation. The idea is not to be on the same level as the competition, but to exceed them. Creativity is everything to an entrepreneur. Some think that creativity and business mix like oil and water, but most successful businesspeople are creative thinkers of their field. Think of Bill Gates, Henry Ford, even the two guys who created Ben & Jerry's—they were all creative thinkers who found a niche in their field. Whether it is design, production, or presentation, being creative is about doing something no one has done before. And remember that all bright ideas come as a surprise.

It's easy to research the competition when you're an online retailer because the enemy is just a click away. What you need to do is keep track of websites that rank high on the search engine results. Also keep track of those that receive a ranking in the top thirty to fifty. This is still considered a decent ranking considering the thousands of websites out there selling the same thing.

My Problem with a Copycat

I have been going head to head with an online competitor for a number of years. This competitor lacks creativity, so much so that they don't even make an attempt to improve on what we've done at PearlParadise. Instead, they copy everything we do.

Like clockwork, every new idea we produce is very closely duplicated. The way we take our pictures, the promotions we hold, even our product description. We started a pearl points program for repeat customers, and they also started a pearl points program—they didn't even bother to change the name of the promotion. We published "8 Pearl Paradise Purchase Points to Ponder" on our home page, and the next week they published "8 Reasons to Buy from Us" on their own site.

Needless to say, this has been very aggravating. But what that other website did helped me realize one important thing: If they are copying us, we must be doing something right. Moreover, as long as they follow, they will never lead—they will always be one step behind.

The Lesson Learned:

To be ahead of your competition, you must be the leader, not the follower. Although it is wise to improve on your competitor's ideas, you must think outside the box on your own as well.

Your Website Is Your Business

When I started PearlParadise.com, there were no other pearl jewelry sites around. I felt comfortable knowing that if someone decided to buy pearls on the Internet, they were likely to buy from me. Unfortunately, this comfort was short-lived. Soon, other pearl sites started to pop up. Most of these pearl jewelry sites were poorly built, and I couldn't really consider them my competition; but there were a few sites that looked very professional, with good price points, good product descriptions, and nice photographs. Although I had the utmost confidence that I sold the best-quality pearls at the lowest price available, it is ultimately the website that sells the product. This meant that I had to rethink the structure and look of my website if I didn't want these other sites gaining the attention of my potential customers. Website modification is something that you will probably have to do from time to time as technology changes and as more sites emerge with better navigational menus.

Sourcing

If you have a good product source, keep it a secret. Don't tell anybody about it, even if you are dying to brag about your success. Moreover, you can think creatively to obtain a new source for your product. You might even think of a new product to buy from your source and market it a new way.

Product Education

Keep abreast of up-and-coming news about your product. Read trade journals and publications. Many are available online. Consistently read the business section of newspapers and magazines, and keep track of market fluctuations. Cut the articles and keep them in a file. You can track the market and product changes this way. Most of all, become an expert on your product.

Product Innovation

You can set yourself apart from the competition by creating a product that isn't available from anybody else in the market. I did this by offering my customers rare pearls that only collectors were privy to in the past.

In the pearl jewelry business, freshwater pearls are very common because they are easily harvested. Freshwater pearls used to account for 20 percent of our total sales. Even though our competition couldn't get relatively close to our source, and even though our buying power kept us in the lead, competitors were able to sell a very similar quality product.

In 2005 I decided to do something that definitely set us apart from our competition. When freshwater pearls are harvested, the farmers separate the best of the best from the good, medium, and poor stock. They do not drill the top-quality pearls for necklaces. Instead, they take the top-quality pearls and sell them one pearl at a time because they can warrant a much higher price.

My idea was to convince several farmers to sell all of their top-quality (loose) pearls to me. I spent nearly a week in Zhejiang province negotiating a price for these gems. When I was finally able to secure them, I contracted a factory to drill these pearls and match them for necklaces. No one had ever done this before on a large scale. I turned all the pearls into necklaces, and the result was a product that only pearl collectors would have had in the past—only now, it was available to the public.

Because I negotiated to buy all the pearls, I didn't pay the huge premium these pearls would typically demand in the open market. Today we are the only pearl site that offers such top-quality freshwater pearls as necklaces. We have no competition in this product niche because no one else has been able to do what I did. But someone will come up with an idea, and it will be back to the drawing board in the brainstorming department for me.

Last Words

If you have a passion for what you do, and you love being in business, then you should have no problem staying ahead of the competition. Striving to be better than anybody else out there is part of the entrepreneurial spirit. Indeed, being in business is like a game, and as with all winners—we all like finishing first!

13 Expanding Your Business

If all goes well, a time will come when you will need to spread your wings and expand your business. The question that presents itself is, when is the right time? That answer is pretty simple: You should expand your business when your sales demand that you expand. You should also realize that there are many ways of expanding your business. Expansion can mean moving into another location, licensing your product, targeting other markets, and/or diversifying your product line. If you've outgrown your home space due to inventory and personnel, then it's time to think about renting an office space. Or you could add product to your line of items for sale. You could even establish an offline retail store.

Research shows that businesses that grow too quickly end up going under. Why? Usually because the business can't sustain the financial pressure involved in expansion. Sole proprietors find that the growth of their business is not enough for them to handle alone. The job and financial responsibility can be overwhelming when sales suddenly increase and there is not enough working capital to sustain the added expense. Partners often tend to disagree about certain business decisions, and this can result in the dissolution of the business. Corporations might not be able to attract the needed investors to raise the capital necessary to finance the growth. Most businesses make premature decisions about selling and/or expanding without properly evaluating the consequences and profitability of the decision.

The Right Time to Grow

In chapter 10 I mentioned a *Newsweek* article that changed my business tremendously. Indeed, my sales increased at such a fast rate that I knew within a month that it was time to move to a business office. My small apartment was no longer sufficient to store my inventory and the staff that I now required.

When I started my business it was a part-time endeavor. I sometimes even thought of it as a hobby; I had considered myself fortunate to have a good business with steady sales. After the article hit the newsstands, the national recognition I received catapulted me from a small-time operation into a nationally recognized business. You might say that I rode the wave of that *Newsweek* article, and I've been fueling the wave ever since. I had always planned to grow, but sometimes business growth cannot be calculated in terms of when and at what point in your life growth will facilitate itself. There will come a time when you will be faced with the choice of expanding. The most important thing to remember when making your decision is why you went into business in the first place. A financial or business consultant can assess your business and its capabilities to help you decide if expansion is right for you. You also need to assess yourself and your capabilities. Ask yourself what you feel comfortable doing, what you are willing to learn, and what aspect of the business just doesn't interest you. You need to find out what you are willing to put into the business in order to determine if expansion is right for you. This self-assessment will also help you determine what type of personnel you will need to add if you choose to expand.

Expanding your business isn't just about increasing product offering, increasing inventory, or hiring new people. Business expansion also means that your function in the business changes. You will have greater financial responsibility and an increased level of commitment. These important factors must be considered in determining whether or not growth right is for you.

Extra Expenses in Business Growth

- Rental space
- Salaries
- Inventory
- Equipment (computers, printers, etc.)
- Additional phone lines

To Grow or Not to Grow

If you're faced with the opportunity to expand your business, the question to ask yourself is whether you actually want to expand your business. Perhaps you went into business for yourself to be your own boss, to have flexible hours, or to be able to work part time. Regardless of your reason, business expansion is not necessarily for everybody. Maybe you want to keep your business a part-time effort because you have other priorities, or maybe you don't want to relocate to a commercial office space because you like the convenience of working at home. With that in mind, ask yourself the following questions:

- Are your sales experiencing a steady increase that is beginning to require that you hire extra personnel?
- Is your home space no longer a viable place to run your business effectively?
- Are you willing to commit the extra time needed to manage a growing business?
- Do you have adequate working capital to finance the needed expenses in an online business?
- Do you plan to add to your product line?

Now that you've asked yourself these basic questions, you need to assess your answers. Perhaps your business has garnered some national attention and you've experienced an increase in sales. You don't want to change your current lifestyle, yet the orders are pouring in! Who would say no to this situation? Believe it or not, some people don't want the added responsibility of having a full-time home-based online retail business. Maybe you want to spend more time with your children or you have other interests that you want to nurture. Maybe your online business is just a side activity whose growth you want to control. If this sounds like you, then you will have to take certain measures to ensure that your business stays as is. If you've established a loyal list of customers, you can retain the current status of your business by just nurturing your business relationship with your current customer base. You can also hold off on marketing, advertising, and/or promotional efforts.

However, if your focus is to grow your business, then keep in mind that the process of growth is not always about the bottom line; it is also about increasing, enriching, and expanding your scope and domination of the market that you have chosen to reign.

Things to Consider in Expanding Your Business

- Capital
- Sourcing for new vendors
- Manpower
- Time investment
- Relocation
- Product line expansion
- Changing legal structure of business

The Pros and Cons of Expanding Your Business

There are various reasons for expanding your business, though not all of them are good. Business expansion can be a very personal issue because the implications of such a change affect not only you, but others as well. The following is a list of advantages and disadvantages:

Pros

- Increased profits
- Product diversity
- Increased market domination
- Pride
- Peer respect
- Fulfilling your dreams

Cons

- Increased investment
- Lack of manpower to handle the extra work
- Business restructuring
- Increased legal implications
- Increased responsibilities
- Business relocation from home to office

For every pro in business growth, there is a con. When your sales increase, it also means additional investment in product inventory and whatever items and/or manpower that will need to be acquired to execute the task efficiently and effectively. Diversification also means added investment in product and the chance that new additions to your product line might not sell as well as other items. Before you expand your product line, make sure that you do the necessary market research to understand the market trend, product demand, and any other developments that will affect the availability, salability, and profitability of your product. Capturing your untapped market means that you have the chance to increase your market share, and increasing your market share means that you must align the capabilities of your business with the emerging market demand for your product.

If you're a sole proprietor, you might think about acquiring a partner or becoming a corporation to increase the capital of your business. But if you do this, it also means that you will have to familiarize yourself with your new business structure and adjust the operations of your business accordingly. The legal implications of growing a business also must be considered. Increasing sales can also mean an increase in your product liability. The more people order from you, the higher your chances are of encountering that one customer who will slap you with an unreasonable lawsuit (see chapter 5).

Relocation is another issue that can be either a pro or a con. If your business suddenly takes a downturn, you are stuck with your rental lease agreement. There are pros and cons to any issue in business, but if you know the implications, you can protect yourself accordingly and even prevent problems from arising.

Passing Up an Opportunity

The opportunity to grow your business can be planned or it can come by sheer accident. In my case, I had always run my business with the intention to grow by increasing my sales. I paid special attention to price, quality, and customer service to ensure that my customers returned to my site. I believe that this is the sure and steady way to grow a business, along with learning to budget and save your capital in the event of a depression in the market or an unexpected expense in the business. I had planned on growing slowly but surely.

However, in 2001 I was faced with an opportunity that looked too good to pass up. I received a call from Sam's Club, a national chain. Sam's Club sells everything from food to wine, from books to CDs, and from clothing to cleaning supplies. At this time, I was beginning to make a name for myself, and Sam's Club was beginning to develop its own jewelry section. My low prices were phenomenal, and Sam's Club found out about my site, perhaps through the various articles being written about me. They realized that I would be a very good source for their pearl jewelry because of my prices and reputation. They called me about possibly supplying their 437 store locations with pearl jewelry.

They arranged a meeting with me at their corporate headquarters in Arkansas. Before I met with them, I was under the impression that they were interested in having me supply them with a variety of pearls in various qualities. When I arrived at the meeting, they were actually interested in only my top-quality pearls. You might think that would be a "gem" of a deal; however, what I immediately realized was that although I could source the quantity they demanded, it would deplete my inventory—all of my top-grade quality pearls would go directly to Sam's. Again, I thought about the money involved in both the sales and investment aspect. Had I gone through with the deal, it would have meant that my business would suffer because I wouldn't have been able to offer my online customers top-quality pearls. I wasn't willing to make that trade-off.

As much as I wanted to take advantage of the opportunity, my first priority was the well-being of my business. The increased sales in supplying Sam's Club didn't justify the compromise to my online business. Growth with the Sam's deal wouldn't have been conducive to my long-term plan, which was to grow my business and develop a reputation in the online retail world. I have never regretted my decision.

A New Business—A New Life

This book has given you the basics of starting a home-based online retail business, but now that your business is up and running, it is time to focus on creating a balance between your personal and professional life. Remember that you embarked on this venture for profit, and that profit is not only about dollars but the overall quality of your life as well. Although your business might be your passion, it is also important to maintain a healthy life outside of your business by making sure that the other parts of your life are not neglected.

Creating a balanced life is important because the rigors of having a business will tend to consume your thoughts and activities. It is a good idea to sit back and reevaluate your priorities. I started my business because I have always had that entrepreneurial spirit of wanting to create something out of nothing, and I wanted to make that creation work for me financially. But the underlying reason I started my business is that I just wanted the best that life and my ability to achieve my dreams could offer me. But success has its price. Do not think that a successful business will make you happy. Your personal life and professional life must work synergistically. If things are wrong in your personal life, your business will tend to suffer, and vice versa. Life has its ups and downs, and the only thing we can do about it is try our best to minimize the downs. There will be times when your preoccupation with work will take its toll on your personal life, and there will be times when your need to have fun and focus on your personal commitments and responsibility will affect your business. Balance is the harmonious co-mingling of the various aspects of your life. This is sometimes not easy to achieve, but it is possible.

The Early Days

In the early days I wasn't really sure where my business would take me. My family and friends viewed my business more as an "idea" than as a solid plan. Even I saw it more as a hobby with potential than as a full-time job.

It was difficult at first, and it took a lot of dedication and time management because I was, in effect, working two jobs. As a flight attendant for Northwest Airlines, I was used to relaxing during layovers and making plans to go sightseeing and exploring. But all that changed when I started my business. Instead of relaxing during layovers, I had a full work schedule planned that involved processing orders, talking to customers on my cell phone, and doing the basic paperwork involved in my daily business activity. Keeping my job with Northwest offered me a steady source of income and gave me a sense of security because I did not depend on my business as my only means of support. But working two jobs eventually took its toll on me. I finally had to choose between the safe bet (my job with the airline) and my passion—my business. I took the risk and followed my passion full time.

The Middle Years

I left a solid job for a business that, although doing very well, did not provide any guarantees for the future. And the disappearance of a steady paycheck and a steady job sometimes made my heart skip a beat. It was a rocky time. Up until then, success had seemed to come in waves. Some months had been good, others were okay but not great—I never knew how much money I'd earn from month to month. Nevertheless, giving up my job with the airline turned out to be the best move I could have made for my business. The additional time I had to focus on the business actually increased my business substantially. Within two months I was doing quite well, and all my doubts and fears were laid to rest. Business was good, and finally making the decision to fully commit myself to my dream changed my whole life.

Being a one-man operation during those years was hectic, but I loved being in control of everything. However, as my business grew, I realized that I couldn't do everything myself. I needed help. Hiring my first employee during these middle years alleviated some of my daily responsibilities, but it also made me look at my business in a completely new way. As a one-man operation I was responsible only for myself. Now that I had an assistant, I was responsible for another person's livelihood, and my attitude about my business rose to an even more serious level. I now had to make sure that everything I did was with the intention of building a solid foundation so that I could remain in business for the long haul. Having to pay someone a salary added a bit of stress, but it ultimately took away a lot of stress. The addition of an employee helped facilitate further growth because I was able to concentrate on other areas of my business such as marketing and product development.

Words of Wisdom

"Balancing is the discipline that gives us flexibility."

—*M. Scott Peck, MD,* The Road Less Traveled

My Business Now

Having a home-based online retail business was great. I was never late to work, I had no overhead—and I really liked my boss. As my business grew, so did my dedication and passion. My creative juices were fueled, and I got heavily involved in various creative marketing techniques to build my business. In early 2003 I finally decided that it was time to rent an office space. The business was steadily increasing, and hiring more people was conducive to the growth of my business. My home space was no longer an effective environment to conduct my business in an efficient manner. Moreover, the busier my business became, the more I realized that I needed to separate my home environment from my business environment. Every home-based business will reach a point when the home environment is no longer a functioning work space or a viable space to nurture business growth. My decision to rent was partly influenced by my need to hire numerous employees. Moving the business from a home environment to a professional office environment had its drawbacks, but it also made me feel that I finally had a legitimate business. Of course, in retrospect, my business has always been legitimate, but moving to a rented space really changed things. I had to be at work on time, job duties had to be specifically laid out, and a formal system had to be developed to make sure that the various people involved in the daily business activities functioned without conflict. A business is a living entity that is constantly changing, and adapting to that change, whether it is internal or external, is part of business survival.

Moving into an office environment and managing a team of employees completely changed my personal life as well. While working from home my business and personal life were deeply intertwined. I was at work while I was at home, yet home was my work, so in a way I was always working. When I needed to get away, I would simply forward calls to my cell phone, walk to the beach, and enjoy the Southern California weather. Moving into the office was a shock to my system. My home was now my oasis of calm, and I was not nearly as free to cast work to the wind and enjoy the weather on the beach.

Creating Balance in Your Life

Running a business does not mean that you have more time. In fact, you might find that you have less time to spend on the things you enjoy. This is especially true if you have a family. You might also find that there is less time to spend with friends. Make sure that you sustain your relationship with family and friends because they are not only important in your life, they can also be your support system. Your passion and dedication in starting a business has probably transferred all your energy to the professional aspect of your life, and in the beginning this might be a good idea. But do not forget that you also need some down time. Whether it involves going to a ball game, reading a book, or having dinner with friends you care about, it is important to have a life outside of business. You will be surprised to find that spending time away from your business will leave you reenergized. Sometimes away time is good for feeding the creative juices. My afternoons on the beach were not only relaxing, they also gave me time to think, which led to creative ideas that I always excitedly carried back to my office.

If you have had an especially hectic work day, take some time to just relax. Try to clear your mind of the issues at work. The time away might give you a new perspective in solving the problem.

Being in Control

Most people think that having a business means that they are always in control. The answer is yes and no. Yes, being your own boss means that you can schedule your daily activities according to your own specifications, and you essentially only have to answer to yourself. However, some business owners do not realize that if your business is successful, you have more people to answer to. You have customers who will be e-mailing you questions about products, prices, and shipments. You will have vendors to deal with as well as the various service representatives you need to keep your online business going. Your employees will turn to you for answers about certain aspects of their daily business duties. There are also fluctuations in the online retail market, product availability, and pricing that are sometimes out of your control. Keeping abreast of market trends, technology, and the competition will help you manage the fluctuations of the industry. Dealing with these types of problems can take time away from focusing your energy on other aspects of growing and maintaining your competitive edge. Moreover, the time it takes to deal with these things can take a toll on your personal life. Problems in business can make you nervous, angry, and irritable. The worst thing you can do is vent on those around you because it only creates feelings of hurt and resentment, and it does not really resolve the problem at hand.

Being in control is about keeping calm in times of chaos. Let me remind you about **PEP: P**repare for the worst, **E**xpect the worst in order to **P**revent the worst from getting the best of you. Planning is key to surviving the uncontrollable forces that sometimes dictate the course of the business world, whether it is online or offline.

Effective Time Management

I remember a time when I thought that having a business meant that I could finally have that extra time to do the things I enjoy. As I mentioned earlier, working as a flight attendant and running a business while I was on layover meant that I could not enjoy the pleasures of wandering new towns, enjoying four-star amenities, and socializing with crew members at the hotel bar—a way of life to which I had easily become accustomed. Being a business owner can consume a lot of your time, and you will sometimes feel that twenty-four hours is just not enough for one day. Building a business can take over your personal life. One way to organize your time is to plan a detailed schedule of business activities that will work with your home life. For instance, you can prepare a to-do list of business and personal tasks and organize them by priority. This is especially true for business owners who have children.

If the kids have after-school activities, you can take your work with you while you are waiting for them. Or you can have your spouse or significant other help you in taking the kids to their practice and/or club meetings. Being a business owner means becoming a master of multitasking and dedicating your time wisely. And time spent with family is always time well spent.

Relationship with Family and Friends

Maintaining a healthy relationship with family and friends and keeping an open line of communication with them regarding what's going on with the business will help alleviate misunderstandings and hurt feelings. Let your spouse or significant other know that despite your recent preoccupation with your business, his or her presence in your life is important to you. Even if you have less time to spend with them, it does not mean that you cannot spend quality time together. Take some time away together to reenergize your relationship. This lets them know that they are still a significant part of your life and that you are willing to do what it takes to nurture that relationship.

Children especially can feel neglected when your energy is focused on building a business. It is especially hard for young children to understand why you are not as available to them as you used to be. Arrange a special activity time for your child so you can regularly spend time together.

If you're a single parent, you have an even greater challenge when it comes to balancing work and family. Keep an open line of communication with your children. Let them know that they are still your number one priority and that your new business is not only for you but for them as well.

Friends

It is important to keep good friends. But friends who do not understand your new preoccupation with something productive are not out for your best interest. Having fun is fine, but you have other priorities now. Again, keep an open line of communication with your friends. Those who care about you will understand.

Personal Time

It's important to have time to yourself. With the busy schedule involved in having your own business, some down time is necessary to regroup your thoughts. We all tend to neglect our health when we're busy, but it's such an important issue—without your health, you wouldn't be able to enjoy the things that you have accomplished. I know that I've stressed the idea of working hard to build your business, but there is a point when you just have to stop and relax. The worst thing you can do to your business is get sick. Establishing an inner peace at certain times of the day can also help you cope with the chaos of being a business owner.

Guidelines and Priorities

Balancing your personal life and your business life sometimes requires the juggling of priorities. Write down your personal and professional priorities, listing them in order of importance. In creating this list, think of your everyday workweek and then consider any special events (weddings, birthdays, anniversaries, parent–teacher conferences, etc.) that require your presence. Also consider potential busy seasons for your business. Remember that your business will be at its most hectic during the holiday season, so keep in mind that you might have to work extra hours processing and shipping orders. This exercise will help you gain perspective on your business and personal situation, and it will also help you juggle your commitments. On the facing page is a form that you can fill out to list your daily activities and to help you approximate how much time you'll need for each.

The form on page 192 should help you prioritize your daily activities. After filling out the Daily Activities form, list your personal and business tasks in the appropriate columns on the Task Schedule. If two tasks coincide, the "Options" section is your opportunity to reschedule one of the tasks for another time or to delegate the duty to someone else. This is a good way to keep yourself organized, and it will also minimize the chaos that tends to ensue when you have a busy schedule.

Words of Wisdom

"Judge your success by the degree that you're enjoying peace, health, and love."
—*H. Jackson Brown Jr.*, Life's Little Instruction Book

Daily Business Activities

1.

2.

3.

4.

5.

6.

7.

8.

9.

10.

Daily Personal Activities

1.

2.

3.

4.

5.

6.

7.

8.

9.

10.

Task Schedule

Time	Business	Personal	Options
8:00 a.m.			
9:00 a.m.			
10:00 a.m.			
11:00 a.m.			
12:00 p.m.			
1:00 p.m.			
2:00 p.m.			
3:00 p.m.			
4:00 p.m.			
5:00 p.m.			
6:00 p.m.			
7:00 p.m.			
8:00 p.m.			
9:00 p.m.			
10:00 p.m.			
11:00 p.m.			
12:00 a.m.			

Final Words

In this book, I have given you an A to Z approach to starting and managing a home-based online retail business. I've given you my success stories, but I've also given you some horror stories, and I've told you how I overcame the trials and tribulations of being an online entrepreneur. I hope that I've answered some of your questions and erased the mystery behind e-commerce. Being a business owner is a lot of work, but it is by far the best thing I've ever done for myself and for those I care about. I now have the financial security I've always dreamt of, and I do take great pride in my achievement. I've worked hard for it.

If I can do it, you can do it too. You don't need any special talent to succeed in this business; you just need a good work ethic, a curious mind, and passion for what you do. Regardless of what you are doing now or what you've done in the past, there is something about your past experience that can lend itself to your business. Don't ever think that you don't have what it takes, because if you have the drive, the desire, and the dedication to become a successful entrepreneur, then you will become one. And if you are innovative, motivated, and pay attention to the marketplace, then nothing can stop you from achieving your dreams. I won't wish you luck because luck has nothing to do with it. It's all about you and what you want to accomplish. Remember that dreaming and doing are a wonderful combination.

Appendix A: Degrees and Certifications

The following schools offer bachelor's and master's degrees in business with an emphasis on e-commerce.

American University

4400 Massachusetts Ave. Northwest

Washington, DC 20016

www.american.edu

Admissions e-mail: admissions@american.edu

Averett University

420 West Main St.

Danville, VA 24541

www.averett.edu

Admissions e-mail: admit@averett.edu

Bellevue University

1000 Galvin Rd. South

Bellevue, NE 68005

www.bellevue.edu

Admissions e-mail: info@bellevue.edu

Brenau University

500 Washington St. Southeast

Gainesville, GA 30501

www.brenau.edu

Admissions e-mail: wcadmissions@lib.brenau.edu

California State Polytechnic University–Pomona
3801 West Temple Ave.
Pomona, CA 91768-2557
www.csupomona.edu
Admissions e-mail: generalinfo@csupomona.edu

Castleton State College
86 Seminary St.
Castleton, VT 05735
www.castleton.edu
Admissions e-mail: info@castleton.edu

Champlain College
163 South Willard St.
Burlington, VT 05401
www.champlain.edu
Admissions e-mail: admission@champlain.edu

City University
11900 Northeast First St.
Bellevue, WA 98005
www.cityu.edu
Admissions e-mail: info@cityu.edu

Clarkson University
Box 5605
Potsdam, NY 13699
www.clarkson.edu
Admissions e-mail: admission@clarkson.edu

Davenport University
415 East Fulton St.
Grand Rapids, MI 49503
www.davenport.edu
Admissions e-mail: Davenport.Admissions@davenport.edu

Ferris State University

1201 South State St. CSS201

Big Rapids, MI 49307

www.ferris.edu

Admissions e-mail: admissions@ferris.edu

Hawaii University at Hilo

200 West Kawili St.

Hilo, HI 92720-4091

www.hilo.hawaii.edu/academics/

Admissions e-mail: uhhadm@hawaii.edu

Holy Family University

9701 Frankford Ave.

Philadelphia, PA 19114-2094

www.holyfamily.edu

Admissions e-mail: undergra@holyfamily.edu

King College

1350 King College Rd.

Bristol, TN 37620

www.king.edu

Admissions e-mail: admissions@king.edu

La Salle University

1900 West Olney Ave.

Philadelphia, PA 19141

www.lasalle.edu

Limestone College

1115 College Dr.

Gaffney, SC 29340-3799

www.limestone.edu

Admissions e-mail: admiss@limestone.edu

Maryville University of St. Louis
13550 Conway Rd.
St. Louis, MO 63141-7299
www.maryville.edu
Admissions e-mail: admissions@maryville.edu

Messiah College
1 College Ave.
Grantham, PA 17027-0800
www.messiah.edu
Admissions e-mail: admiss@messiah.edu

Methodist College
5400 Ramsey St.
Fayetteville, NC 28311-1498
www.methodist.edu
Admissions e-mail: admissions@methodist.edu

Seattle University
901 12th Ave.
Seattle, WA 98122-4340
www.seattleu.edu
Admissions e-mail: admissions@seattleu.edu

Stetson University
421 North Woodland Blvd.
Deland, FL 32723
www.stetson.edu
Admissions e-mail: admissions@stetson.edu

Texas Christian University
2800 South University Dr.
Fort Worth, TX 76129
www.tcu.edu
Admissions e-mail: frogmail@tcu.edu

Tiffin University

155 Miami St.

Tiffin, OH 44883

www.tiffin.edu

Admissions e-mail: admiss@tiffin.edu

University of La Verne

1950 Third St.

La Verne, CA 91750

http://laverne.edu

Admissions e-mail: see their online form

University of Maine–Fort Kent

23 University Dr.

Fort Kent, ME 04743

www.umfk.maine.edu

Admissions e-mail: umfkadm@maine.edu

University of North Texas

PO Box 311277

Denton, TX 76203

www.unt.edu

Admissions e-mail: undergrad@unt.edu

University of Pennsylvania

3451 Walnut St.

Philadelphia, PA 19104

www.upenn.edu

Admissions e-mail: info@admissions.ugao.upenn.edu

University of Scranton

800 Linden St.

Scranton, PA 18510-4694

www.scranton.edu

Admissions e-mail: admissions@scranton.edu

University of South Alabama

307 University Blvd.

Mobile, AL 36688-0002

www.southalabama.edu

Admissions e-mail: admiss@usouthal.edu

University of Southern Indiana

8600 University Blvd.

Evansville, IN 47712-3596

www.usi.edu

Admissions e-mail: see their online form

Vanderbilt University

2201 West End Ave.

Nashville, TN 37235

www.vanderbilt.edu

Admissions e-mail: admissions@vanderbilt.edu

Community College

Community College of Beaver County

1 Campus Dr.

Monaca, PA 15061

www.ccbc.edu/exploring/locations.jsp

Offers Advanced E-Commerce Certificate

Certificate Offered Credits Required: 30

Online College

University of Phoenix

170 locations nationwide

www.universityofphoenix.com

Offers bachelor's and master's degrees

Appendix B:
Recommended Reading

Accounting

Ivens, Kathy. *QuickBooks 2006: The Official Guide.* Columbus: McGraw-Hill, 2005.

Kimmel, Paul D. *Financial Accounting: Tools for Business Decision Making.* Newburgh: Wiley, 2003.

Business

Alterowitz, Ralph. *Financing Your New or Growing Business: How to Find and Get Capital for Your Venture:* Entrepreneur Press, 2002.

Drucker, Peter F. *The Daily Drucker: 366 Days of Insight and Motivation for Getting the Right Things Done.* New York: HarperCollins Publishers L.L.C., 2004.

———. *The Essential Drucker: The Best of Sixty Years of Peter Drucker's Essential Writings on Management.* New York: HarperCollins Publishers L.L.C., 2003.

Gregory, Kip G. *Winning Clients in a Wired World: Seven Strategies for Growing Your Business Using Technology and the Web.* Hoboken: John Wiley & Sons, Inc., 2004.

Home Office

Barrett, Niall. *The Custom Home Office: Building a Complete Workspace.* Newtown: Taunton, 2002.

Kanarek, Lisa. *Home Office Solutions: Creating a Space That Works for You.* Bloomington: Quarry, 2004.

Inspirational

Brown, Bruce. *Another 1001 Motivational Messages and Quotes.* Monterey: Coaches Choice Books, 2003.

Copeland, Gary, et al. *Motivational Selling: Advice on Selling Effectively, Staying Motivated and Being a Peak Sales Producer.* Tulsa: The Ozols Business Group, 2004.

Vilord, Thomas J. *1001 Motivational Quotes for Success: Great Quotes from Great Minds.* Cherry Hill: Garden State Publishing, 2002.

Internet Law

Brinson, Dianne J., et al. *Internet Law and Business Handbook: A Practical Guide* (Diskette). Chicago: Independent Publishers Group, 2000.

Darrell, Keith B. *Issues in Internet Law.* College Station: Virtualbookworm.com, 2005.

Feinman, Jay M. *Law 101: Everything You Need to Know About the American Legal System.* New York: Oxford University Press, 2000.

Ferrera, Gerald, et al. *Cyberlaw Text and Cases.* New York: South-Western College, 2003.

Hiller, Janine, et al. *Internet Law and Policy.* Englewood Cliffs: Prentice Hall, 2002.

Isenberg, Doug. *Giga Law Guide to Internet Law.* New York: Random House, 2002.

Rustad, Michael L., et al. *E-Business Legal Handbook.* New York: Aspen Law & Business, 2002.

Marketing

Barletta, Martha. *Marketing to Women: How to Understand, Reach, and Increase Your Share of the World's Largest Market Segment.* Chicago: Kaplan Business, 2006.

Hanson, Ward. *Internet Marketing and E-Commerce.* Mason: South-Western College, 2006.

Kleindl, Brad. *Strategic Electronic Marketing: Managing E-Business.* Mason: South-Western College, 2002.

Levinson, Jay C. *Guerrilla Marketing: Secrets for Making Big Profits from Your Small Business,* 3rd ed. New York: Houghton Mifflin, 1998.

Meyerson, Mitch. *Success Secrets of the Online Marketing Superstars.* Chicago: Kaplan Business, 2005.

Roberts, Mary L. *Internet Marketing: Integrating Online and Offline Strategies.* Columbus: McGraw-Hill, 2002.

Rubino, Joe R. *The Ultimate Guide to Network Marketing: 37 Top Network Marketing Income-Earners Share Their Most Preciously-Guarded Secrets to Building Extreme Wealth.* Hoboken: Wiley & Sons, Inc., 2005.

Product Sourcing

Kurlantzick, Joshua. *"On Foreign Soil: Arm Yourself with the Information and Advice You Need for Sourcing Your Product Overseas So Your Efforts Don't Get Lost in Translation."* Entrepreneur *33,* no. 6, p. 88.

Website Design and Development

Nettleton, Nick. *How to Design and Build the Coolest Website in Cyberspace: Hot Design Solutions for the Coolest Site on the Web.* New York: Ilex, 2003.

Writing

Cook, Claire K. *Line by Line: How to Edit Your Own Writing.* Boston: Houghton Mifflin, 1986.

Eisenberg, Brian, et al. *Persuasive Online Copywriting: How to Take Your Words to the Bank.* Austin: Wizard Academy Press, 2002.

Stilman, Anne. *Grammatically Correct: The Writer's Essential Guide to Punctuation, Spelling, Style, Usage and Grammar.* Cincinnati: Writer's Digest Books, 1997.

Strunk, William Jr., et al. *The Elements of Style.* New York: Longman, 2000.

Zinsser, William K. *On Writing Well, 25th Anniversary: The Classic Guide to Writing Nonfiction.* New York: Collins, 2001.

Appendix C:
Internet Terminology

ADSL (Asymmetric Digital Subscriber Line): A DSL line where the upload speed is different from the download speed. Usually the download speed is much greater.

Apache: An HTTP server software most common on the Internet. This is a free web server that was instrumental in the growth of the WWW, and it continues to be the basis for the design of other web servers.

Applet: A Java program that can be inserted in an HTML page. It is a program that runs within another program.

Application Server: A server software that manages other software packages, enabling them to be accessed by a web server.

Bandwidth: How much information you can send through a connection. Usually measured in bits per second (bps). A full page of English text is about 16,000 bits. A fast modem can move about 57,000 bits in one second. Full-motion, full-screen video would require roughly 10,000,000 bits per second, depending on compression.

Bit (Binary Digit): A single-digit number, either a 1 or a 0. A bit is the smallest unit of computerized data. Bandwidth is usually measured in bits per second.

Blog: A website that provides postings by users in chronological or reverse order. Postings are usually about a particular topic of interest.

Broadband: Generally refers to a method of signaling that works with different frequencies.

Browser: A software program that allows the user to look at and display web pages on the WWW.

Byte: A set of bits that represents a single character. Usually there are eight bits in a byte, sometimes more, depending on how the measurement is being made. In programming language, a byte is a basic integral data type.

Cache: A computer storage mechanism that remembers previously accessed information for faster retrieval.

Cookie: Messages (text files) that a web browser sends to a web server, usually to track a user's activity on the web.

Cyberspace: A term used to refer to the WWW or the resources available on the Internet.

DHTML (Dynamic HyperText Markup Language): DHTML refers to web pages that use a combination of HTML, JavaScript, and CSS to create features (including features that let the user drag items around on the web page, produce some simple kinds of animation, and more).

DNS: Also known as Domain Name System. DNS deciphers domain names into IP numbers.

Domain Name: An internet address or site. (For example: www.yahoo.com.)

Download: Transferring or copying a file (data) from one computer to another or from one source to your computer.

DSL (Digital Subscriber Line): Moves data over phone lines at a high speed.

E-mail (Electronic Mail): Messages sent from one source to another through a computer.

Ethernet: A very common method of networking computers in a LAN.

FAQ (Frequently Asked Questions): FAQs are documents that list and answer the most common questions on a particular subject. There are hundreds of FAQs on subjects as diverse as pet grooming and cryptography. FAQs are usually written by people who have tired of answering the same question over and over.

Fire Wall (or Firewall): A system used to prevent unauthorized Internet users from accessing information from a private network. A firewall is a protection device used to navigate the traffic in a computer network in trusted areas (internal network) and areas of no trust (Internet).

Frames: Frames divide web pages into various scrollable areas.

FTP (File Transfer Protocol): A procedure for transferring or exchanging files over the Internet. The most common use of FTP is for downloading files to a server using the Internet.

Gateway: A hardware or software that serves as an entrance or access to another system.

Gigabyte: 1,000 megabytes.

Hit: Retrieval of an item (web page) from a web server. In search engines a hit refers to the number of times a website matches the keywords or search condition of a particular inquiry.

Home Page (or Homepage): The main page of a business or personal web page.

Host: A computer system that contains data that can be accessed by a remote terminal. A host can also mean the entity that provides web space.

HTML (HypterText Markup Protocol): The language used in documents for the WWW, usually a series of tags and codes.

HTTP (HyperText Transfer Protocol): A protocol used to transmit and format document data for the WWW.

Hypertext: The linking of data and images through text on the WWW. Hypertext within a written document on the WWW is usually highlighted or underlined so that the user can click the word and be taken to another web page.

ICANN (Internet Corporation for Assigned Names and Numbers): A nonprofit corporation based in Marina Del Rey, California, responsible for developing various Internet policies such as domain name allocation.

Inbound Links: Inbound links are hyperlinks from other websites or web pages that go to your site.

Internal Links: Links within your website that connect to another website or web page.

Internet: The total global collection of interconnected computer networks. Internet in the lowercase ("internet") refers to the connection of network computers.

Intranet: An interconnection of computer networks within a private company.

IP Number (Internet Protocol Number): An IP number can be considered the web address of a particular website much like the address of a house or business.

ISP (Internet Service Provider): An institution that provides access to the Internet.

Java: A programming language, developed by Sun Microsystems, used in the WWW.

JavaScript: JavaScript is a programming language that is mostly used in web pages, usually to add features that make the web page more interactive.

JPEG (Joint Photographic Experts Group): Used to format file images.

LAN (Local Area Network): A computer network specifically for a limited area.

Login: The account name used to gain access to a computer or online account, or the act of connecting to a computer or online account.

Megabyte: One million bytes.

Meta Tag: An HTML tag with information about a web page that is invisible to the viewer of the web page.

Modem: A device that allows a computer to transmit data over phone lines. Cable and DSL connections also require modems.

Network: A connection of two or more computers for the purpose of sharing and communicating data.

Outbound Links: Hyperlinks from your website that go to another website or web page.

Password: A code made up of a series of characters that allows a user to gain access to a computer, file, e-mail, or web page.

PDF (Portable Document Format): A file format developed by Adobe Systems that allows a file to be viewed in its original hard-copy format.

Portal: A website that functions as the first site an Internet user will see when using the web. Portals have various features and resources such as search engines, e-mail, and shopping.

Posting: A message in a website bulletin board or blog.

Protocol: A series of rules that is agreed upon by two systems in transmitting and receiving data.

Proxy Server: A server that allows indirect connections to other network servers. It provides an indirect connection between the real server and a web browser in order to process a request before giving it to the real server. Used as a means of filtering the request and reducing the time of accessing a website if another user has previously requested the website.

Search Engine: A system for searching keyword information on web pages on the WWW.

Security Certificate: A chunk of information (often stored as a text file) that is used by the SSL protocol to establish a secure connection.

SEO (Search Engine Optimization): A method for increasing the page ranking of a website in search engines.

Server: A computer or software package that manages network resources.

Spam: Unsolicited e-mail.

Spyware: A software program that secretly monitors the websites a user has visited on the WWW without the user's knowledge.

SSL (Secure Socket Layer): A protocol designed by Netscape Communications to enable encrypted, authenticated communications across the Internet.

T-1: A leased-line (connects the two connections) connection to the Internet capable of carrying data at 1,544,000 bits per second.

Tag: A language used in creating web documents (includes commands to determine how text should be read by a search engine).

Upload: Transferring data or files from a computer to another network. Uploading is the opposite of downloading.

URL (Uniform Resource Locator): The first part of a domain name (HTTP or FTP) that indicates what protocol to use.

Virus: A chunk of aggressive programming code that unilaterally makes copies of itself, typically to send to other computers using your system as a host. A virus can enter your computer without your knowledge and detrimentally alter the way your computer operates.

Web: Short for "World Wide Web."

Web Page: A document designed for viewing in a web browser. Typically written in HTML, a website is made up of one or more web pages.

Website: The location of a web page in the WWW.

Wi-Fi (Wireless Fidelity): A popular term for a form of wireless data communication. Basically, Wi-Fi is "Wireless Ethernet."

Worm: A worm is a virus that does not infect other programs. It duplicates itself and infects additional computers (typically by making use of network connections), but it does not attach itself to additional programs; a worm might alter, install, or destroy files and programs.

WWW (World Wide Web): The information available through web pages on the Internet.

XHTML (eXtensible HyperText Markup Language): Basically, XHTML is HTML expressed as valid XML. XHTML is intended to be used in the same places you would use HTML (creating web pages), but it is much more strictly defined, which makes it a lot easier to create software that can read it, edit it, check it for errors, etc.

Appendix D:
Frequently Asked Questions

There are so many things to do when starting an online retail business. What should I do first?

Find a product that you know you can sell. Without a good product, your business will never be successful—no matter how nice your site is. Make sure your product can be sold online. In other words, if you sell a $5.00 item that weighs 40 pounds, the low-value-to-high-weight ratio makes this an inappropriate product to sell online. Good online products have a high value-to-weight ratio. Do some research to find out who else is selling the product. If you can offer customers a better deal or offer the product in an innovative way, then you have established a product niche for yourself.

What is the biggest obstacle in starting an online retail business?

It is difficult to get customers to your website if they don't know about it. You can build a great site and sell a great product, but if no one knows your company name, you will not sell any product. Making your site visible involves search engine optimization techniques and an effective online marketing strategy.

What is the most common misconception about being a business owner?

Most people think that being a business owner immediately makes you rich. We have all heard the business dreams/plans of our friends and relatives. How many of these dreams come to fruition? Starting a new business is a lot of work, and great success rarely comes overnight, but if you're tenacious, patient, and hardworking, it is possible to be a successful online business owner.

How can I product-source overseas if I don't speak the language?

Deal with suppliers who speak your language, hire an interpreter, or take the initiative to learn the language.

How much inventory should I buy in the beginning?

If the inventory is easy to source, only buy what you need to get started. Make a sales projection to determine how much inventory you will need.

What is the difference between a home-based online retail business and selling on eBay?

Owning your online business is much more secure than eBay, and the credit card transaction fees are lower than eBay's. If you sell on eBay, you don't really own your own online business, and one policy change at eBay can destroy your entire business.

Should I keep a hard copy of business-related material, or can I just store everything in my computer?

Never store everything you need on your personal computer. There are two inevitable elements in owning an online business: taxes and computer failure. Your computer will eventually give you trouble, and if you have not saved your business data, you will likely lose a portion of it. I do not necessarily recommend saving hard copies of all your business dealings, unless the business does not have a large number of transactions. It is easier to save your data on disks or on a separate hard drive that you should keep in a location away from your home office.

Is it wise to consult with an attorney before embarking on an online business?

I think it is always wise to consult with an attorney before venturing into any new business arena. Most, however, do not do this when starting a home-based business. If the reader has already signed up for legal insurance, I would suggest consulting an attorney, free of charge, before proceeding.

What are the most important questions to ask an attorney when it comes to Internet retail laws?

Trademark/copyright questions, tax collection and liability, and import/export restrictions (in the event you source from or sell to overseas markets) are very important topics to discuss with an attorney.

How has the WWW changed in the ten years you've been in business?

When I started in business, the Internet was still small. There was actually a book called *The Internet Yellow Pages*. This book, which was the size of a phone book, purported to contain the addresses of most of the world's websites. It would take the Library of Congress to house all the names of today's websites.

Also, people were not accustomed to shopping online when I started. I had to convince people that shopping online was actually better than going to the store. This is now commonly accepted, but it was not ten years ago. I convinced customers with my customer service policy (guarantees, return policy) and my prices that shopping at my online store was worthwhile. My goal was to show them that there was only one reason they should not walk into a jewelry store to buy pearls again—me!

How will online retail change in the next five years?

More people will shop online. Unfortunately, while consumers will become more accustomed to online shopping, more unscrupulous characters will also try to steal from consumers and vendors alike. I believe that the next trend on the Internet is going to be in shopping security (fraud prevention) to provide more protection to the consumer and the merchant.

What is more important on a retail website—graphics or content?

Content is king! While graphics can add an aesthetic quality to your site, content is definitely more important. Without content, search engines cannot find your site during a search, and people will not know that your site exists. Besides, unnecessary graphics can annoy customers, and they can slow down some computers when their file sizes are too large.

Should I hire a writer to write product descriptions?

This depends on you, really. I did not hire a writer for my product descriptions, but I did hire a writer for my personal biography and the "About Us" page on the site. I feel comfortable about writing content because I'm a pearl expert, but I did not feel comfortable writing my own biography, so I hired a professional writer.

If you do not feel that you are a good writer, it is best not to write your own content. But if you do write your own content, use keywords in the beginning of the site as titles or headings. If you are writing articles, use spell-check and grammar-check extensively. Spelling and grammar problems will hurt your credibility and search engine rankings.

How much technical information about website design do I need to know if I plan to have a professional build my site?

You do not need to know a lot, but I would recommend learning as much as possible. If you learn, you will not be at the mercy of your designer's time. You will be able to make small changes when needed, and you will know more of the capabilities and inner workings of your site. You can never have too much information.

What are the most common programs used for web design?

Dreamweaver, Adobe Photoshop, and Adobe Go Live are some of the most popular programs to use in website design.

Is it a good idea to buy website design software if I plan to commission a website designer to create my website?

I suggest that you buy the programs so that you are able to learn how to make changes to the site yourself. As you progress in your business, you will eventually have to learn the programs yourself or have an employee make changes for you. Contract workers are a bit more difficult to depend on—they work for themselves, not for you. So, in the long run, it is better to update your website yourself or in-house.

What should I look for when hiring a web designer?

Thoroughly examine other websites the designer has built. Call the owners of the sites to gauge their experience with the designer. Research the sites on search engines such as Google and Yahoo to ensure that they show up in search engines. If the designer does not create search engine–friendly sites, you should not hire him.

What is the average cost of building a website?

If you design the site yourself, building it will not cost much. If you hire a designer, you can have a site built for as little as a few hundred dollars (I hired a designer to build Pearl-Guide.com for $400) or you could spend thousands. I had Pearl Paradise.com rebuilt several years ago and spent approximately $10,000 for a professional designer.

At what point in my business should I obtain pay-per-click advertising?

Pay-per-click advertising may be your only initial method of advertising. But any pay-per-click campaign must be carefully monitored to ensure that you have a positive ROI (return on investment). If you have a 5 percent conversion rate (5 percent of the visitors purchase) and you are paying $1.00 per click on the search engines, then you are paying $20.00 for each customer. Your profit margin must support your conversion rate. You can increase your conversion rate by making the customer feel more confident in the site, providing more pertinent information, and bettering the navigability of the site.

Should I choose a service provider that offers pay-per-click advertising?

Although there are currently several pay-per-click companies today, the only two that I can recommend are Google and Yahoo. All others, in my experience, do not drive good traffic to your site, and the traffic that is directed to your site does not convert as well as Yahoo and Google traffic.

Should I have articles on my website about the products I'm selling?

Yes. Content about the product you're selling gives the impression of credibility and helps your site rankings. Do not, however, copy another site's content page. Duplicate content—content that can be found elsewhere—is unoriginal, and customers (who have looked at sites selling the same or similar products) will know that you have copied the work. You want to establish yourself as an expert in your field, and you won't do that by copying content. Much more important than this is the fact that if search engines find duplicate content on your site, they will not rank your site well, and at times they will not rank it at all.

For example, I once helped someone develop a website to sell pearls that he was buying from me. I gave him a lot of direction, and he developed a nice site. However, at the last stage he decided to cut corners and copy text from another site to use in his "pearl information" section. This killed his chances of ever having a successful site. His site was essentially blacklisted from the top search results. The search engines viewed his site as a regurgitation of previously published information. It was impossible for his site to rank well. Remember that good content increases your search rankings and establishes trust in the eyes of your customer. But the content must be unique—I cannot stress this enough.

What was your first successful marketing strategy?

The customer-only sale was my first successful marketing strategy. I decided many years ago to try to capitalize on my existing customer base. Pearls are not something that you would expect people to buy over and over again. But they do, with the right marketing and promotion. I decided to develop a "past-customer-only" sale. I built a special page on my website twice a year and sent a link to this "secret" page to all past customers (I still do this twice a year). This page contains pieces available in limited quantity and priced as low as possible—typically very close to cost. Many of the pieces I offer are pieces or types of pearls that I stumble upon over the course of the year (pieces I have purchased far below market wholesale value, typically by luck). I am able to sell these pieces at prices so low that I would not want to advertise them on my main website. The past customers love this, and this has made many of them lifelong customers.

Start-up businesses seem to have no leverage when it comes to negotiation with vendors and various service providers. How can I make negotiations work for me if I have no leverage?

Shop around. Do not implicitly trust every vendor you meet. Shop around for others, and use their prices and services against each of them. Leverage is something you build up, but you do not want to start in a poor position. Suppliers are typically very friendly, but they are rarely your friends in the beginning. Their goal is to give you as little as possible for as much as possible. Your goal is the polar opposite.

How difficult is it to obtain an online merchant credit account provider if I have a high-risk business?

It is not difficult to obtain a provider; it will simply be more difficult to obtain a good rate. In general, an Internet-based retail business is considered high-risk in and of itself, because fraud is a serious issue online.

When researching online merchant credit account providers, how can I tell a reputable company from a bad one?

Look at their customers and speak with them. Check with the Better Business Bureau to see if they have had complaints lodged against them. Research them as much as possible. Definitely "Google" them thoroughly.

How does a bad credit history get in the way of starting an online retail business?

A bad credit history may affect the rates you are able to obtain from a merchant processor. Your credit will also affect any loans you may apply for and credit from many vendors.

Should I have a marketing brochure printed if my business is online?

If you plan to market offline, a marketing brochure may be useful. We have a "press kit" that is quite large. We also have a "company backgrounder," which is tri-fold with pictures and information on each page. We include only the most pertinent information in this piece. We typically give both of these to members of the press that we meet.

From a marketing standpoint, how effective is free shipping?

Free shipping can be very effective for many businesses. But I feel that it really depends on the type of business you are in. I have seen a gamut of sites that offer free shipping, and they all sell pearls. However, these sites that offer free shipping do not have higher conversion rates than my site, which does not offer free shipping because we offer the lowest prices and have established credibility. People are more concerned with a good value for their money and a quality product from a credible website than saving the $5.00 for shipping. If you are selling a standard item where quality may not be an issue (DVDs or books), free shipping will certainly increase your conversion rate.

How much capital should be invested in marketing and/or advertising?

I cannot give you a solid figure on this. It really depends on the product and your overhead. You must be careful how you spend your money. There are many, many companies out there that will happily take your money, promising great success. There are very few, however, that will actually provide. Stay away from the following:

- Banner ads (offering you a number of banner ad placements for a set fee).
- Search engine inclusion (offering to submit your site to hundreds of search engines). There are only three search engines that really matter (Google, Yahoo, and MSN), and your inclusion is based on the quality of your site, not the number of times you have been submitted.
- Links in "shopping malls." There are several companies that will place a link to your website in thousands of "online malls" around the world. What they do not tell you is that these sites really receive no traffic. They are a waste of money!

- Opt-in lists are offered by companies that will send your message to thousands of potential clients who have opted to receive information from companies like yours. They are basically offering to spam people for you—this would be business suicide.

Do spend your marketing budget on honest search engine optimization (as provided by www.localsubmit.com, the company chiefly responsible for the efficacy of my search engine optimization). Also spend your budget on public relations campaigns when the time is right. Issue online press releases about what your company is doing.

How can I establish word-of-mouth buzz on my product?

Give your customers something to talk about. Make their experience memorable and exciting. If they cannot remember the name of your company a week after the purchase, even if they love the product, you have lost an opportunity for new customers. Treat each customer as if they were your only customer—show a genuine interest in them. They will remember these extra touches.

How important is self-promotion in marketing?

Very important, but it can be quite difficult. I suggest hiring a public relations representative or a public relations firm to promote you. I think this is the most important marketing tool, although it can be quite expensive. If you cannot afford a public relations representative, learn how to initiate your own PR campaigns. If your campaign is successful, it will likely bring success to your business.

At what point in my business should I hire a public relations firm for self-promotion?

Hire a PR firm as soon as you can afford one. But you must have a story to tell, or you may be wasting your money. The hiring of a PR firm and the optimization of my site were, financially, the two best moves I have made in business.

How can I keep my prices competitive?

Keep your overhead low and source well. Remember, online shoppers love to shop around. If you are selling a widget and there are 100 other companies online selling the same or similar widgets, customers are likely to purchase from a more reasonably priced site or a seemingly more credible site (all other factors being equal).

If I'm selling discounted items on my site, is it a good idea to display the average retail cost of a product?

Absolutely. It is important to display the average retail price. Customers must know that they are getting a deal and that they are not purchasing substandard merchandise. The retail prices must be realistic, however. eBay has developed a bad image in the online jewelry sector, as it places few controls over the advertising of its members. It is common to see jewelry items selling on eBay for less than $50 with advertised retail prices higher than $5,000. Not only is this illegal (although eBay does nothing to stop it), it hurts eBay's credibility when merchants place inaccurate prices on their products.

How can I beat the competition if our price points are practically the same?

Your site should be easy to navigate, searchable, and have an overall ease of usability. Use focus groups to determine how user-friendly your site is, and compare your site to your competition. Focus groups can consist of friends or family—people you trust to give you an honest opinion. Beat the competition with the usability of your site and the pre- and post-sale service.

- Pre-sale service: Make yourself available to customers. Have a toll-free number. Answer customer e-mail questions with expedience.
- Post-sale service: Check back with your customers to make sure that the product has met or exceeded their expectations. Be available via telephone or e-mail for any concerns or questions your customers may have.

You will be surprised how many companies are all about customer service before the sale. But after the product and money have changed hands, it is easy for a company to feel as though its job is done. Good post-sale service will leave a lasting impression on your customers.

When is the right time to move my business from home to an office?

I cannot say there is ever a right time. I would definitely say that if you need to hire employees, you should probably take the business out of the house.

When is it a good idea to sell my business?

Never—unless you are no longer satisfied with your business. Your business will become a part of you—a family member of sorts. Stress and hardships are part of owning a business and part of having a family.

Index

insurance, 27
  product liability, 82
Internal Revenue Service, 74
Internet, 86
Internet checks, 157
Internet terminology, 204
irs.gov, 74

J
JavaScript, 111

K
keywords, 106

L
lawsuit, 49, 78
legal issues, 77
liability, 50
licenses, 47
Limited Liability Company, 59
limited partnership, 54
link farms, 105
linking, 108
litigation, 78
localsubmit.com, 105
logo, 79

M
management summary, 62, 65
marketability, 29
marketing, 118
  objectives, 120
  through website, 131
  yourself, 133
market research, 14, 118, 123, 182
market summary, 62, 64
MasterCard, 148, 154, 157
media planning, 123, 135
merchant account, 147

merchant account providers (MAP), 147
meta tags, 104, 108, 110
middleman, 39
mitigation, 78
money orders, 148, 157
MSN, 88, 99, 217
multitasking, 17

N
negligence, 81
negotiation, 41
networksolutions.com, 21
niche, 19, 29
Nielsen Rating, 126

O
office supplies, 25
offline advertising, 120
online retail business
  characteristics needed for running, 6
  differences from brick-and-mortar store, 18
  pros and cons, 9
  reasons for success and failure, 6
  skills, 11
online transactions, 149
optimization, 86, 103
organization, 75
ownership, 50

P
package tracking, 165, 168
packaging, 170
partnership, 51
pass-through taxation, 51
payment gateway, 150
payments, 147
PayPal, 149–150, 154
pay-per-click advertising, 107, 120
permits, 47

About the Author

Jeremy Shepherd is the founder of the multimillion-dollar online empire PearlParadise.com. Since 1996 PearlParadise.com has become the leading online pearl wholesaler and retailer in the world. Jeremy's inspirational story and the success of PearlParadise.com have been featured in numerous radio stories, magazines, and newspapers including the *Wall Street Journal, Newsweek, Entrepreneur, In Style,* and *Modern Bride.* The 78th Academy Awards selected PearlParadise.com as part of their Oscar Gift Basket for the second year in a row. Jeremy has also conducted interviews on various television shows such as *Extra* and *Entertainment Tonight.*

A vacation to China ignited Jeremy's passion and interest in pearls. He realized that buying directly from the pearl farmers in China eliminated the middlemen, and he immediately saw the market potential. His expertise in pearls and his entrepreneurial instincts led him into the online wholesale/ retail business, where his talent for discovering the profitability of a product through savvy marketing strategy launched PearlParadise.com.

Jeremy has a bachelor's degree in business and marketing, he is a GIA (Gemological Institute of America) graduate with a certificate in pearls, and he speaks five languages. He became fluent in Spanish and Japanese while in his teens, and he speaks Chuuk, the obscure language of the South Pacific Micronesian Islanders. His Berlitz training in Mandarin became very useful during his numerous visits to China.

Jeremy's intense desire for knowledge is an important factor in his success, along with the philosophy that credibility, honesty, and common sense are key ingredients in creating a profitable online business. His inspirational and motivational story proves that it is possible to grow a successful business by doing something you love.

About the Revisor

Nicole L. Augenti was born and raised in New York City. The practice of law is what brought her to Connecticut. She is an attorney in Bridgeport Connecticut. She is a sole practitioner at her law firm, Law Offices of Nicole L. Augenti, LLC which she founded in 2009. In addition to operating her own law firm, Nicole continues to work as an independent contractor for Attorney James O. Gaston after serving as his legal assistant from 2000 through 2009. Nicole is a litigator who practices in the area of personal

Photo courtesy of Carolyn Heimann

injury, representing clients who are victims of automobile collisions, premises defects, products liability, medical malpractice, and other forms of personal injury. Nicole is a passionate advocate of the civil justice system, and works tirelessly to secure justice for her clients.

She was the founding member and President of the Association of Trial Lawyers of America (ATLA) now known as the Association for Justice (AAJ) Student Chapter and Member of the Probate Journal from 2004-2005 at Quinnipiac University School of Law, from where she received her Juris Doctor in 2008.

Now, as an attorney, she has been appointed as a Member to the Marketing and Client Services Committee of AAJ in 2011. Her knowledge of social media and background in e-commerce were factors in her appointment to this position with AAJ. Nicole did her Undergraduate work and graduated (Cum Laude) from Pace University with a B.S. in Criminal Justice in 2003. She is a current member of the Connecticut Bar and is admitted to practice in the U.S District Court, Connecticut. She is a member of the American Association for Justice, the Connecticut Bar Association and the Connecticut Trial Lawyers Association.